A Brief Introduction to

– LaTeX–

Oliver Sternal

Impressum
Bibliographic information published by the Deutsche Nationalbibliothek: The Deutsche Nationalbibliothek lists this publication in the Deutsche Nationalbibliografie; detailled bibliographic data are available on the Internet at dnb.dnb.de.

Published by: BoD · Books on Demand GmbH,
Überseering 33,
22297 Hamburg,
bod@bod.de

Printed by: Libri Plureos GmbH,
Friedensallee 273,
22763 Hamburg

ISBN: 978-3-6963-7545-4

Translated from the German original with AI assistance and human review.

About the Author and the Book
Oliver Sternal holds a PhD in physics and has been teaching regular introductory LaTeX courses for over 20 years. The lecture notes for these courses, originally developed between 2006 and 2009, were first released as an e-book and have now been revised for this print edition.

"A Brief Introduction to LaTeX" is specifically aimed at beginners who have had no prior experience with LaTeX and are looking to take their first steps. The book provides a straightforward introduction to the language and its fundamental elements.

FSC
www.fsc.org
MIX
Papier aus verantwortungsvollen Quellen
Paper from responsible sources
FSC® C105338

Contents

Preface

The typesetting system LaTeX and its many companions have become indispensable in the daily professional life of STEM fields. It is frequently required as the standard for writing lab reports, theses, and scientific publications in renowned journals. Consequently, LaTeX is one of the essetial soft skills that many scientists and engineers must acquire during their studies. While some are fortunate enough to attend organised courses, others must sit down independently at home with a book or an online guide to teach themselves.

This book originated between 2006 and 2009 as a lecture script for various LaTeX courses I taught during that period. I hadn't originally planned to publish it. It was only that after I began offering introductory LaTeX courses again recently – still using "A Brief Introduction to LaTeX" as my primary teaching material – that I decided to revise and release it.

I hope this book can make a small contribution by providing you an overview and sparking a deeper interest in LaTeX. To be clear from the start: "A Brief Introduction to LaTeX" is not a comprehensive reference manual and will not guide you into every depth that an expert, extensive literature, or online research could. The goal of these lecture notes is to facilitate your entry into working with LaTeX and to repeatedly remind you how essential search engines, online forums, and AI tools are for working effectively with the system.

Speaking of the internet and AI tools: Even though you can write LaTeX documents more conveniently using an online editor or even have an artificial intelligence generate them for you, it remains essential to master LaTeX yourself and, above all, to be capable of drafting scientific texts independently. When writing a thesis, you will often handle data – potentially highly sensitive – that should not be shared before official publication[1] or may even need to be kept confidential[2]. If you use an online editor or an AI tool (one that is not university-hosted and shielded from the outside world), you could run into serious trouble.

After this lengthy introdution, I suggest we dive right into the core of the book. I wish you much enjoyment and, above all, great success with the projects for which you require LaTeX.

Oliver Sternal

[1]... because, for instance, your entire career depends on ensuring your research findings are linked to your name and published through an official, reliable channel.

[2]... for example, when collaborating with a company in the private sector, where developements, data, and operational procedures may be classified as trade secrets.

Chapter 1

Introduction

1.1 What is LaTeX?

LaTeX is a typesetting system that handles the layout and structuring of a document based on predefined standards. In commercial word processors, these tasks typically require manual adjustment. Using LaTeX, text, tables, and images are automatically arranged to fit the document optimally. Similar to HTML, the content and structural instructions are defined in a source file, which is later converted into a readable format using a compiler.

1.2 Why Learn LaTeX?

At first glance, LaTeX may seem like a complicated language that is demanding to learn and time-consuming to apply. However, once you have understood its underlying principles, using it becomes easier and more convenient than any commercial software. The significant advantages in typesetting mathematical formulae, generating indeces (especially bibliographies) and cross-references, as well as the harmonious and consistent appearance of a LaTeX document, can hardly be achieved in any other way with so little effort and such high quality. Thus, it is no surprise that LaTeX has established itself as the standard in the scientific community for writing lab reports, Bachelor's and Master's theses, dissertations, and publications in scientific journals.

Another strength lies in its vast range of applications: (almost) any type of document can be created with LaTeX. Simple articles, books, letters, posters, and even Beamer presentations represent only a small selection of what is possible.

This introduction covers only a small fraction of this vast selection. You will also not find any in-depth technical descriptions here. Instead, this book is intended as a catalyst for engaging with LaTeX. Naturally, references to further reading will be provided. Perhaps the most important advice for aspiring LaTeX users is therefore given right here: search engines, internet forums, and AI tools are a LaTeX user's best friends. Almost every problem you could possibly imagine in LaTeX has almost certainly already been tackled by someone somewhere in the world and, in many cases, discussed in internet forums. If you cannot find a direct solution, you should post you problem in a forum. Typically, you can expect a qualified answer in a very short amount of time.

1.3 Software and Installation

The software required to work with LaTeX is available for free download on the internet. Since a printed book cannot ensure that the information on the latest software developments — and especially the download links — remains up to date, only a few brief notes are provided here.

To create or edit LaTeX documents, you will require:

1.3.1 A LaTeX Distribution

Open your web browser and choose a search engine. Entering "LaTeX" along with the operating system installed on your computer should provide you with an adequate selection. Two widely used distributions at the time of this book's publication are *MiKTeX* and *TeX Live*. Follow the download instructions on the respective website and install your chosen LaTeX distribution according to the directions. You can usually choose between two options: a full installation (recommended if you work extensively with LaTeX without an internet connection) or a partial installation (recommended if you are more or less always connected to the internet). The partial installation initially takes up little disk space but grows over time, as additional packages are only downloaded and installed when they are needed.

1.3.2 A Comfortable Editor

A specialised LaTeX editor allows you to create a readable document from the LaTeX source code at the touch of a button. A good editor offers *syntax highlighting*, which makes it easier to maintain an overview of your source code by highlighting text passages and commands according to their properties. Well-known examples include *TeXnicCenter*, *TeXworks*, or *Texmaker*.

1.3.3 Overleaf and the Overleaf Problem

In many courses, working with *Overleaf* is recommended. In this book, however, the use of the online editor *Overleaf* or other online editors is explicitly discouraged. This is due to two reasons:

1. **Error Tolerance**
   Even though *Overleaf* uses a standard TeX-Live distribution, the settings are configured such that *Overleaf* "forgives" a large number of errors and still generates a PDF. A locally installed distribution, on the other hand, will halt the compilation process and fail to produce a PDF file. If you use *Overleaf*, the ability to identify and correct errors will not become part of your skill set.

2. **Data Privacy**
   At the latest when you write a thesis or a scientific publication, you will be processing data and content that should not be distributed uncontrollably throughout the world. This is especially true if you are completing a thesis (Bachelor's, Master's, or Doctoral thesis) in cooperation with companies from the private sector. However, even papers written at the university contain research results that should not leave the university's internal domain before they are published in a thesis or a scientific article.
   By storing this content on an international server where you do not know what happens to your data, you may encounter data protection, disciplinary, and/or commercial law issues. This must be avoided at all costs.

If you nevertheless and despite all warnings feel the urgent need to work with *Overleaf*, please note that the generation of a PDF file in *Overleaf* does not mean that your source code is error-free. Pay close attention to *Overleaf's* error output and eliminate all errors. (Note: Warnings are not errors.)

1.3.4 Programs for Viewing Created Documents

From a LaTeX source code, you can create various readable, platform-independent formats. The most well-known among them is certainly the *Portable Document Format (PDF)*, closely followed by *PostScript (PS)*. If you intend to work exclusively with one of these two formats, you only need one program to view that format. However, it does no harm to install options for both formats.

Download all the programs you need for free from the internet. This is, by the way, one of the major advantages of LaTeX compared to other software. In the context of LaTeX, you should not engage with any websites or other providers where you have to pay for the acquisition.

During installation, it is essential to ensure that you install the editor as the last program. Most editors automatically search for software associated with LaTeX and configure themselves accordingly. If you install the editor first, you will usually have to handle the configuration yourself.

1.4 Literature for Free Download

To learn and deepen your understanding of LaTeX, a vast collection of books is not necessary. Sufficient free literature is available via the internet to dive deeper into the subject matter and to experiment with a variety of different things. At this point, a small selection of documentations is listed, which are also referenced elsewhere in this book and which partly served as sources for the author. The respective documents can be found using any internet search engine by entering the title, the file name, or a keyword.

The Comprehensive LaTeX Symbol List (Scott Pakin)
The *Comprehensive LaTeX Symbol List* is a compilation of several thousand different characters and symbols, including descriptions of how to generate each of them.
(File: symbols-a4.pdf)

Math Mode (Herbert Voß)
The *Math Mode* documentation describes how to work with mathematical environments and formulas.
(File: Mathmode.pdf)

Documentation for amsmath (American Mathematical Society)
The *amsmath* package offers numerous useful extensions for math-

ematical symbols and environments.
(File: amsldoc.pdf)

BibTeXing (Oren Patashnik)
The correct use of bibliographies and citations is becoming increasingly important nowadays, as several prominent cases in recent years have shown. Of course, LaTeX in combination with *BibTeX* or *BibLaTeX* can assist with this as well.
(File: btxdoc.pdf)

PSTricks User's Guide (Timothy Van Zandt, Denis Girou)
The *PSTricks* User's Guide is an introduction to using the *PSTricks* packages for creating graphics with LaTeX. Although we will not cover this package further in this book, this manual is a valuable resource for alternatives.
(File: pstricks-doc.pdf)

TikZ and PGF Manual (Till Tantau)
TikZ is a standard method for creating graphics with LaTeX that is powerful and flexible. We will explore this package extensively in this book.
(File: tikzpgfmanual.pdf)

The Beamer Class (Till Tantau, Joseph Wright, Vedran Miletic)
This comprehensive guide introduces the use of the beamer class for creating presentations.
(File: beameruserguide.pdf)

Chapter 2

Creating a Simple Document

Let us begin our introductory course with an entry into the elementary framework of this extensive subject. First, some fundamentals are required before we can start creating documents. Let us therefore first take a look at how a LaTeX document is structured and which elements it consists of.

2.1 Commands, Environments, and Groups

LaTeX documents are constructed using commands that describe what should happen to the source code when the document is converted. These commands are preceded by a backslash \ so that they can be distinguished from "normal" text. They provide instructions for the subsequent characters in the source code or represent a specific character themselves.

It often makes sense to treat an entire part of a text as a group of words. This is enclosed in curly brackets `{group of words}`. If a command is placed before the leading bracket, this command applies to the entire group. You will find several examples of this process in this documentation.

In addition, environments are frequently required to give their content very specific properties. Examples include mathematical formula environments, tables, or lists. The typical structure of such an environment consists of its beginning, the content and its end:

```
\begin{environment}
  %
  the content
  %
\end{environment}
```

2.2 The Structure of the Source Code

Similar to a website written in *HTML*, LaTeX source code is clearly designed. (Allow me a small remark here: this naturally depends on the author. It should rather be said: the source code should be well-structured and clearly organised.) It is divided into a *header* (preamble) and a *document body*. While all important definitions are made in the header or preamble, the content is located in the document body between `\begin{document}` and `\end{document}`. This results in a practical separation of design specifications and content, allowing for quick changes to the content-independent properties of the entire document.

2.2.1 The Header (Preamble)

The header of a LaTeX document contains the information required for the *document layout* and the *command sets* used. This is where the *document class* (see below) is defined, individual *packages* providing new commands, characters, and environments are specified, or new commands themselves are defined. The Header contains all information LaTeX needs to convert the source code into a "real", readable document that meets the author's requirements.

2.2.2 Document Classes and Packages

The structure of the document is determined by the *document class*. The first command in the source code tells LaTeX whether you want to write an article, a book, or a Beamer presentation:

```
\documentclass[options]{document class}
```

This is how you choose the layout and, in many cases, obtain specific commands tailored to that class.

article is one of the most frequently used document classes. It is intended for shorter articles. Its structure begins with the `\section` (see below).

report is used for longer articles. Here, the structure can be divided into chapters (`\chapter`), and a title page is automatically created.

book facilitated writing books through its special presets. It allows for `\chapter` division and starts every new chapter on an odd-numbered page. A title page is automatically created. There is a specific adjustment of the margins tailored to bookbinding.

slides helps in creating overhead transparencies through specifically adapted structures and font sizes.

beamer is the ideal replacement for commercial programs to design presentations.

a0poster enables the – not always entirely straightforward – design of posters up to DIN A0 size using LaTeX.

minimal is – as the name suggests – a class with minimal predefinitions. It was created to serve as a starting point for developing new document classes.

When selecting a class, additional options can be specified directly to define the design. If no further options are provided, the respective default settings of the classes are used. Since additional specifications are often useful or even essential, some possibilities are presented here:

Paper format
In LaTeX all common formats can be selected. Some examples are `a4paper`, `a5paper`, `b5paper`, `legalpaper`, `executivepaper` or `letterpaper`.

Font size
The font size is specified in points, e.g. `8pt`, `9pt`, `10pt`, `11pt` or `12pt`. The font sizes that can be used, as well as the standard setting (default value), depend on the document class used. For some document classes that use specific font sizes, this specification is ineffective.

Print format

You can choose between single-sided (`oneside`) and double-sided (`twoside`) printing. This option influences, among other things, the setting of the margins. (An important setting, especially for documents that are to be bound after printing.)

Chapter start

In a book, a chapter usually begins on an odd-numbered page. This setting can be changed by selecting `openany` or `openright`.

Draft version

The options `draft` and `final` output either a preliminary version without graphics but markers for overfull lines, or a final version of the document.

Title page

Wheter a title page is created – or not – can be forced using `titlepage` or `notitlepage`.

Furthermore, so-called *packages* are required, which help to achieve additional settings for the document – such as the input character set used in the source code or the language in which the document is to be written. These are included in the header after the selection of the document class using the self-explanatory command:

```
\usepackage[options]{package name}
```

Some importang packages are briefly introduced here:

babel along with a language option (e.g., `english` or `ngerman`) defines the language in which the document is written.

inputenc declares the character set used in the file containing the source code. The current standard is the `utf8` option, which is set as the default.

fontenc specifies the font encoding used in the converted, readable document. The `T1` option is the standard font encoding and is selected automatically unless this package is loaded with a different option.

graphicx enables the integration of graphics. Please note that not every graphics format can be used. If you convert LaTeX source code into a *PostScript* document, only the graphics formats *PostScript* and *Encapsulated PostScript* can be included. If, on the other hand, a *PDF* document is generated from the source code, the formats *JPEG*, *PNG*, and *PDF* can be included.

multicol enables the typesetting of the document in multiple columns. This can be particularly helpful for documents in landscape format and especially when creating posters.

amsmath and amssymb provide extensions to the mathematical environments and expand the list of mathematical symbols that can be used.

longtable overcomes the limitation of writing tables over a maximum of one page, thereby enabling long tables to span multiple pages.

color offers colour output and provides various predefined colours for this purpose.

microtype takes care of many micro-typographical refinements that may not be noticeable at first glance.

Usually, documentation is provided with every package, explaining exactly which additional properties and commands the LaTeX document acquires through its use. If the documentation was not installed along with the LaTeX package, it can be found by entering the *name of the package* with the suffix *documentation* into any search engine.

2.3 A Simple Example

After having struggled through the basics up to this point, let's write a first small example using a simple standard header. To do this, let's open our LaTeX editor and enter the following lines:

```
\documentclass[a4paper,12pt]{article}
\usepackage[english]{babel}
\usepackage[utf8]{inputenc}

\begin{document}
Hello World!
\end{document}
```

Note: While *a4paper* is the standard in Europe and most parts of the world, you may want to use the *letterpaper* option if you are writing specifically for a North American audience.

In this short source code, we can subsequently enter and test all commands and packages. For the sake of clarity, the header and the `\begin{document}` and `\end{document}` commands will be omitted in all following examples, unless they are required for a better representation of a specific example.

This source code must now be saved. To do this, you should first create a new directory where all files belonging to the document you are writing will be stored. Click the *save button* in your editor and navigate to the directory where you want to save your source code and the resulting document. Enter a filename of your choice with the `.tex` extension and save the file.

During compilation, LaTeX generates a series of additional log files, which can also be found in this directory. The compilation process will be explained in the next section (see below).

It is often important to describe or mark certain parts within a source code in more detail, or perhaps to leave a remark for a co-author that should not appear in the converted document. In other words: you want to insert a comment. This is done by prefixing a % to the respective line that is to be commented out:

```
Sometimes it happens,
% This is only visible
% in the source code.
that a comment needs
to be inserted.
```

Sometimes it happens, that a comment needs to be inserted.

In the example shown here, you see the source code entered in the editor on the left side. The right side shows the result in the readable document generated from the source code. Most of the following examples are structured according to this same principle: the left side shows a source code, while the right side displays the corresponding result after compilation.

2.3.1 Compiling the Source Code into a Readable Format

For some time now, there has been a whole range of specialised LaTeX editors where the conversion into various file formats works automatically at the touch of a button. You can select he output format (usually *DVI*, *PS*, or *PDF*) and finally create the selected document by clicking a button. During this process, LaTeX outputs a log of the compilation process, including warnings and error messages. In the event of errors, good editors will also indicate the line where the program found an error, making corrections much easier. Most editors have a separate window where this output is displayed, as well as buttons that allow you to click through the error messages and warnings.

If everything went well during compilation, the generated output file is placed in the same directory where the source code was saved. Some editors open the output file automatically after compilation or have a corresponding button for this. Sometimes, however, your may have to do this yourself.

2.4 Adding Structure to your Document

Anyone can write a simple text. Now, let's move on to everything that goes beyond that.

2.4.1 Sectioning Commands

All document classes offer the possibility to structure a document. For this purpose, the commands `\section{title}`, `\subsection{title}` and `\subsubsection{title}` are available, with the hierachy already becoming clear through the names of the commands. Furthermore, the `book` and `report` classes offer a higher-level unit `chapter{title}`. In the readable document, the individual sections are numbered consecutively according to their level.

If you want to suppress numbering, you can append a * symbol to the respective command, e.g., `\section*{title}`. However, by doing so, you also accept that the respective part will not initially appear in the corresponding directory – in case of structure, the *table of contents* (or *toc* for short). This can be bypassed relatively easily with the command:

```
\addcontentsline{directory}{sectioning-level}{title}
```

In case of the table of contents, *directory* is replaced by `toc`. Instead of the *sectioning-level*, we enter `chapter`, `section`, `subsection` or `subsubsection`, depending on the structural level that should be included in the table of contents. We illustrate the process using the example of a section:

```
\section*{title}
\addcontentsline{toc}{section}{title}
```

2.4.2 Creating a Table of Contents

Furthermore, LaTeX offers the advantage that a table of contents can be generated from such a structure using the `\tableofcontents` command. However, it is important to note that LaTeX processes the document from the beginning to the end during compilation. During this process, a log file (specifically a `.toc` file) is first created; only during a second compilation can the table of contents be read from this file and fully inserted into the document. Not every LaTeX editor performs this second pass automatically, though some editors will handle this task for you.

The setting `\setcounter{tocdepth}{n}` in the preamble of the LaTeX source file allows you to select the depth to which the table of contents should be displayed. Here, `n` represents an integer (0, 1, 2, ...), indicating how many levels of the document structure below the highest level should appear. (For the table of contents in this book, the setting `\setcounter{tocdepth}{1}` was used. The section level is visible below the chapter level. If `n` = 0 were chosen, only the chapters would be shown; with `n` = 2 subsections would also appear in the table of contents.)

2.4.3 Title, Author, and Date

In the header of the document, the title, author, and the date to be displayed on the title page can be defined. The format of the date depends on the selected language package. If no date is specified, LaTeX automatically uses the date of the day the source code is compiled. These settings are passed to LaTeX using the commands `\title{title}`, `\author{author}`, and `\date{date}` and can be displayed, for example, at the beginning of the document using `\maketitle`. Here is a small example:

```
\documentclass[a4paper,12pt]{article}
\usepackage[english]{babel}
\usepackage[utf8]{inputenc}

\author{John Doe}
\title{The Sense and Nonsense of learning \LaTeX}
\date{22 March 2026}

\begin{document}
\maketitle
Hello World!
\end{document}
```

2.4.4 New Paragraphs, Line Breaks, and Page Breaks

LaTeX documents are usually typeset as justified text, meaning the margins are the same on both the left and right sides of every line. Words in a line are arranged to make optimal use of the available space. Only then is the line broken, with the last word being hyphenated if necessary. The number of spaces between two words or two sentences in the source code is irrelevant, as long as there is at least one:

```
Silly          example
```

Silly example

If you want to force a manual line break or start a new paragraph in LaTeX, you need the appropriate commands, because

```
a line break
in the editor
does not mean
a break in the
document.
```

a line break in the editor does not mean a break in the document.

Rather, the following options are available:

```
A line break or the

beginning of a new\\
paragraph can be\newline
forced in \LaTeX\ with\par
various methods.
```

A line break or the
beginning of a new paragraph
can be
forced in LaTeX with
various methods.

The options shown here have different effects. While the double backslash `\\` and the `\newline` command create a simple line break, a blank line in the source code or the \par command starts a new paragraph. A new paragraph can be recognised (unlike in the example shown here) by the indentation of the line. (You can see this, for instance, in the structure of the book in front of you. Try it yourself with a longer text!)

A new page is started with the command \newpage.

In exceptional cases, unforeseen things can happen at the end of a line. For instance, some words may occasionally be hyphenated in the wrong place. If LaTeX cannot find a hyphenation point for a word, it might even be written beyond the end of the line. These are all things that have no place in a "beautiful" document. To avoid this, you can manually define the hyphenation position of a word.

With the \hyphenation command, you can specify in the document header exactly where certain words are allowed to be broken. However, this command is only valid for words without special characters:

```
\hyphenation{ doc-u-ment hyphen-ation }
```

Inserting one or more \- into a word within the text ensures that, for this specific instance, the word may only be hyphenated at those exact positions. In contrast, wrapping a word or phrase in \mbox{expression} prevents hyphenation altogether:

```
Sometimes you want to
achieve different
hy\-phen\-ations than
those provided by default.
```

Sometimes you want to achieve different hyphen-ations than those provided by default.

```
Some things, e.g., the
date \mbox{2026-03-22},
should not be
hyphenated.
```

Some things, e.g., the date 2026-03-22, should not be hyphenated.

If all efforts to create a reasonable line break with sensible hyphenation fail, sometimes the only way out is to manually increase the priority of a break using the command \linebreak[n], where n is a number between 0 (low priority) and 4 (high priority). The exact opposite can be achieved with \nolinebreak[n]. These options are also available for page breaks using \pagebreak[n] and \nopagebreak[n].

2.4.5 Spacing

Horizontal and vertical spacing comes in several different variants with various lengths:

Non-breaking space (prevents line breaks)	~
Very small horizontal space	\,
Negative horizontal space (reduction)	\!
Horizontal space, as wide as a digit	\enspace
Horizontal space, as wide as a letter is high	\quad
Twice as wide as \quad	\qquad
Horizontal space of length x	\hspace{x}
Vertical space, a quarter of a line	\smallskip
Vertical space, a half a line	\medskip
Vertical space, a full line	\bigskip
Vertical space of length x	\vspace{x}

The commands \hspace{x} and \vspace{x} can be used to create horizontal and vertical spaces of length x, where x must be a length consisting of a number and a unit. For example, \hspace{3mm} creates a horizontal space of 3 millimeters. The units that can be used for specifying lengths in these two commands are shown in the following table:

mm	\vspace{15mm}	Millimeters
cm	\vspace{1.5cm}	Centimeters
in	\vspace{1.5in}	Inches (1 in $\hat{=}$ 2.54 cm)
pt	\vspace{20pt}	Points (1 pt $\hat{=}$ 0.351 mm)
bp	\vspace{20bp}	Big Points (1 bp $\hat{=}$ 0.353 mm)
em	\vspace{2em}	2× width of a digit (or 'M') in the current font
ex	\vspace{2ex}	Hight of the letter 'x' in the current font

2.4.6 Text Alignment

Using the environments flushright, flushleft, and center, you can achieve right-aligned, left-aligned, or centered typesetting without margin justification and without hyphenation:

`\begin{flushright}`
`Right-aligned text`
`\end{flushright}`
	Right-aligned text

`\begin{center}`
`Centered text`
`\end{center}`
	Centered text

`\begin{flushleft}`
`Left-aligned text`
`\end{flushleft}`
	Left-aligned text

2.4.7 Font Sizes

The font size can be manually adjusted later, always relative to the base font size set in the document header. If you use one of the commands shown in the following table at any point in the source code, all subsequent text will be set in the corresponding font size.

`\tiny`	tiny	`\large`	large
`\scriptsize`	scriptsize	`\Large`	Large
`\footnotesize`	footnotesize	`\LARGE`	LARGE
`\small`	small	`\huge`	huge
`\normalsize`	normalsize	`\Huge`	Huge

If you want to return to the normal font size after a few words or sentences, use the command `\normalsize`.

The commands specified here always change the font size relative to the base font size selected for the entire document.

2.4.8 Highlighting Text

Very often, it is necessary to mark or highlight a part of a text. This can be done in several ways:

`\textbf{bold text}`	**bold text**
`\textit{italic text}`	*italic text*
`\emph{emphasised text}`	*emphasised text*
`\textsuperscript{superscript}`	superscript
`{\color{red}red text}, black text`	red text, black text

If the \emph command is used again within another \emph command – meaning certain parts within an already emphasised text segment are highlighted once more – the selected text will be set in upright font again.

The xcolor package is required for colored text. The text to be highlighted can be combined into a group using curly braces. Another option is to switch back to black font color at the end of the colored section.

2.4.9 Footnotes

If you would like to explain a minor detail that doesn't quite fit into the flow of the text, you can work with footnotes[1]. In many academic fields, footnotes are also used for citations. By appending the command \footnote{footnote text} to a term, the term is marked with a consecutive superscript number, and the footnote is automatically placed at the bottom of the page.

2.5 Control Characters, Special Characters, and Symbols

You already know that the backslash \ is used to identify a command. This and several other characters are interpreted as control characters in LaTeX. Sometimes, however, it is unavoidable to use these as normal symbols within a text. Therefore, they are written as commands by prefixing them with a backslash:

\& \% \$ _ \{ \} \#   & % $ _ { } #

The backslash itself is generated using the command \textbackslash.

2.5.1 Hyphens, Dashes, and Ellipses

LaTeX distinguishes between several types of hyphens and dashes. While the long em-dash (---) is uncommon in German, it is frequently used in American English as a dash without surrounding spaces. In contrast, British English typically prefers the shorter en-dash (--) with spaces for this purpose. There is also a specific command for ellipsis points.

[1] This is a particularly creative example of a footnote.

-	--	---	\dots	\ldots
-	–	—	...	...

2.5.2 Quotation Marks

Various types of quotation marks are available in LaTeX. In British English, single quotation marks are typically used for primary quotes, while double quotation marks are used for quotes within quotes:

Single	‘ ... ’	‘ ... ’
Double	‘‘ ... ’’	“ ... ”
Double German	"‘ ... "’	"‘ ... "’
Single French	\flq\ ... \frq	<... >
Double French	"< ... ">	"¡ ... "¿

2.5.3 Umlauts, Accents, and Special Characters

Umlauts, accents, and special letters or symbols can be represented using commands. If you want to place accents over the letters 'i' or 'j', the dots must be omitted. All of this is illustrated in the following table:

ü	\"u	ñ	\~n	è	\`e	ó	\'o
ß	\ss	â	\^a	ç	\c c	ẋ	\.x
s̄	\=s	ǒ	\v o	å	\aa	ẓ	\d x
ı	\i	ȷ	\j	Å	\AA	Æ	\AE
Ł	\L	ø	\o	o̊	\r o	æ	\ae

§	\S	£	\pounds
^	\textasciicircum	¶	\P
•	\textbullet	\	\textbackslash
†	\dag	‡	\ddag
©	\copyright	™	\texttrademark
ⓩ	\textcircled{z}	®	\textregistered

Of course, this table is not exhaustive, but the method for composing various characters should be clear. By including additional packages beyond the standard ones in LaTeX, the set of possible symbols and special characters can be expanded. A good overview is provided, for example, by the *Comprehensive LaTeX Symbol List* (Pakin). Chapter 3 introduces a series of mathematical symbols. For anything further, please refer to the internet and search engines.

Chapter 3

Typesetting Mathematical Formulae

3.1 Fundamentals

One of the major advantages offered by LaTeX is the typesetting of formulae. All variables originating from a formula, various special characters, and, for example, the Greek alphabet are considered mathematical characters. These can be written either directly within the text or in a dedicated math environment.

As part of a text, mathematical symbols and formulae must be placed between `\(` and `\)`, `\begin{math}` and `\end{math}`, or simply between two $ symbols:

```
In \LaTeX, \(\alpha\),
\begin{math}\beta\end{math}
and $\gamma$ are mathematical
symbols.
```

In LaTeX, α, β and γ are mathematical symbols.

As part of a formula, all characters are set in italics. Conversely, it is not possible to write text directly within a mathematical environment without further measures, as all characters would be interpreted as formula symbols. Instead, text can be written inside a mathematical environment using `\mbox{Text}`. However, the font size often has to be adjusted manually in this case. A more elegant solution is offered by the `amsmath` package with the command `\text{Text}`:

`$x=3 \mbox{ or } x=-2$`	$x=3 \mbox{ or } x=-2$
`$x=1 \text{ or } x=-5$`	$x=1 \text{ or } x=-5$

3.2 Important Mathematical Expressions

The following section describes some frequently used expressions:

3.2.1 Exponents and Indices

`x^2`	`a^{2n}`	`r_0`	`k_{\text{sol}}`
x^2	a^{2n}	r_0	k_{sol}

It is good practice to always enclose exponents and indices in curly braces, even when it is not strictly necessary for a single character. This prevents frequent errors when dealing with longer strings of characters.

3.2.2 Roots

`\sqrt{2,5}`	`\sqrt[3]{8}`
$\sqrt{2,5}$	$\sqrt[3]{8}$

3.2.3 Fractions

`\frac{1}{2}`	`\frac{a^{2}+b^{2}}{a^{2}-b^{2}}`
$\frac{1}{2}$	$\frac{a^{2}+b^{2}}{a^{2}-b^{2}}$

3.2.4 Marking Expressions

`\overline{x^{2}+y^{2}}`

$$\overline{x^{2}+y^{2}}$$

`\overbrace{a^{2}+b^{2}=c^{2}}^{\text{Pytagoras}}`

$$\overbrace{a^{2}+b^{2}=c^{2}}^{\text{Pytagoras}}$$

```
\underline{x^{2}+y^{2}}
```

$$\underline{x^2 + y^2}$$

```
\underbrace{a^{2}+b^{2}=c^{2}}_{\text{Pytagoras}}
```

$$\underbrace{a^2 + b^2 = c^2}_{\text{Pytagoras}}$$

3.2.5 Spacing

Horizontal spacing with different lengths:

very small horizontal space	`\,`
reduction of the horizontal space	`\!`
horizontal space as wide as a letter is high	`\quad`
twice as large as `\quad`	`\qquad`

3.3 Math Environments

It is often useful to separate a formula from the text, especially for equations that should be highlighted. For this purpose, there are a number of environments in LaTeX in which mathematical formulae and equations can be written. A simple math environment without numbering is realised using the `displaymath` environment:

```
\begin{displaymath}
x^{2} = 4
\end{displaymath}
```

$$x^2 = 4$$

If you want to provide formulae with a number in order to be able to refer to them more easily in the text, the `equation` environment is helpful:

```
\begin{equation}
x^{2} = 4
\end{equation}
```

$$x^2 = 4 \qquad (3.1)$$

If you want to use the `equation` environment and prevent numbering, this can also be achieved here with the `*`, and the equation is written between `\begin{equation*}` and `\end{equation*}`.

LaTeX offers various possibilities for typesetting multi-line formulae. One, for example, is eqnarray. Here, each line is given its own number. Line breaks are created with a double backslash \\. The lines of the formula can (but do not have to) be aligned with one another using a maximum of two & symbols, which makes the layout more consistent. In particular, when writing a multi-line formula, care must be taken to ensure that there are no blank lines within the formula environment in the source code:

```
\begin{eqnarray}
x^{2} &=& 4\\
x      &=& \pm 2
\end{eqnarray}
```

$$x^2 = 4 \qquad (3.2)$$
$$x = \pm 2 \qquad (3.3)$$

By inserting a * into the name of the environment (eqnarray*), numbering is completely suppressed throughout the entire environment. If you want to prevent this only for individual lines, \nonumber can be placed before the respective line within the formula environment.

Similar results can be achieved using the split environment, which is provided by the amsmath package. This is inserted into a standard equation environment. Exactly one number is then assigned to the complete set of formulae:

```
\begin{equation}
\begin{split}
x^{2} &= 4\\
&= \pm\sqrt[4]{4^{2}}
\end{split}
\end{equation}
```

$$\begin{split} x^2 &= 4 \\ &= \pm\sqrt[4]{4^2} \end{split} \qquad (3.4)$$

3.4 Examples of Mathematical Typesetting

Here are some simple examples of what can be achieved with mathematical typesetting in LaTeX.

3.4.1 Functions

Variables are usually typeset in italics in mathematical formulae. In order to clearly distinguish a function, such as sine or the exponential function, from variables, the convention is that function names are typeset upright. Incidentally, the same applies to indices that are not variables and to units. Therefore, corresponding commands exist in LaTeX for some functions. The use of functions is demonstrated here using the example of a complex number:

```
\begin{displaymath}
z = \cos x + i\cdot\sin x
\end{displaymath}
```

$$z = \cos x + i \cdot \sin x$$

and a limit:

```
\begin{displaymath}
\lim_{n \to \infty}
\left(1+\frac{1}{n}\right) = 1
\end{displaymath}
```

$$\lim_{n \to \infty} \left(1+\frac{1}{n}\right) = 1$$

A more extensive list (which is certainly not exhaustive) can be found at a later point.

3.4.2 Sums and Integrals

A simple example of a sum:

```
\begin{displaymath}
S=\sum_{n=1}^{N}\frac{1}{n}
\end{displaymath}
```

$$S=\sum_{n=1}^{N}\frac{1}{n}$$

Integrals are written in the same way:

```
\begin{displaymath}
I(R)=\int_{0}^{R}r\,\text{d}r
\end{displaymath}
```

$$I(R)=\int_{0}^{R}r\,\text{d}r$$

The `\limits` command places the limits of integration above and below the integral sign:

```
\begin{displaymath}
I(R)=\int\limits_{0}^{R}r\,\text{d}r
\end{displaymath}
```

$$I(R)=\int\limits_{0}^{R}r\,\text{d}r$$

3.4.3 Vectors and Matrices

A vector...

```
\begin{displaymath}
\vec{e}_{r} =
\left(\begin{array}{c}
\sin{\vartheta}\cos{\varphi}\\
\sin{\vartheta}\sin{\varphi}\\
\cos{\vartheta}
\end{array}\right)
\end{displaymath}
```

$$\vec{e}_{r} = \left(\begin{array}{c} \sin{\vartheta}\cos{\varphi}\\ \sin{\vartheta}\sin{\varphi}\\ \cos{\vartheta} \end{array}\right)$$

...can be created just as easily as a matrix:

```
\begin{displaymath}
\mathbf{A} =
\left(\begin{array}{c c c c}
a_{11} & a_{12}  & \ldots  & a_{1M}\\
a_{21} & a_{22}  & \ldots  & a_{2M}\\
\vdots & \vdots  & \ddots  & \vdots\\
a_{N1} & a_{N2}  & \ldots  & a_{NM}
\end{array}\right)
\end{displaymath}
```

$$\mathbf{A} = \left(\begin{array}{c c c c} a_{11} & a_{12} & \ldots & a_{1M}\\ a_{21} & a_{22} & \ldots & a_{2M}\\ \vdots & \vdots & \ddots & \vdots\\ a_{N1} & a_{N2} & \ldots & a_{NM} \end{array}\right)$$

Both are represented by the `array` environment and are placed between `\begin{array}` and `\end{array}`. The number of columns and the column alignment are defined in the curly brackets following `\begin{array}`. A `c` centers the columns one below the other, while `l` or `r` set left- or right-aligned columns respectively. The number of `l`, `r`, or `c` entries in the curly brackets defines the number of columns in the array. A new line is started with a double backslash \. (We will encounter the same structure again when dealing with tables.)

3.5 Mathematical Symbols

Anyone who has taken a closer look at their keyboard will have noticed that the options for entering various characters are severely limited. In particular, the vast number of mathematical symbols cannot be found there for practical reasons alone. And who would want to carry around a laptop with a keyboard measuring several square metres? Searching for the required character on such a keyboard would probably be even more arduous. LaTeX provides a remedy here – as it already does for entering special characters in text – by defining various commands, some of which will now be presented.

3.5.1 The Greek Alphabet

α	`\alpha`	β	`\beta`	γ	`\gamma`
δ	`\delta`	ϵ	`\epsilon`	ε	`\varepsilon`
ζ	`\zeta`	η	`\eta`	θ	`\theta`
ϑ	`\vartheta`	ι	`\iota`	κ	`\kappa`
λ	`\lambda`	μ	`\mu`	ν	`\nu`
ξ	`\xi`	o	`o`	π	`\pi`
ϖ	`\varpi`	ρ	`\rho`	ϱ	`\varrho`
σ	`\sigma`	ς	`\varsigma`	τ	`\tau`
υ	`\upsilon`	ϕ	`\phi`	φ	`\varphi`
χ	`\chi`	ψ	`\psi`	ω	`\omega`
Γ	`\Gamma`	Δ	`\Delta`	Θ	`\Theta`
Λ	`\Lambda`	Ξ	`\Xi`	Π	`\Pi`
Σ	`\Sigma`	Υ	`\Upsilon`	Φ	`\Phi`
Ψ	`\Psi`	Ω	`\Omega`		

3.5.2 Various Markings

$\hat{x}$	`\hat{x}`	$\tilde{x}$	`\tilde{x}`	$\bar{x}$	`\bar{x}`
$\vec{x}$	`\vec{x}`	$\dot{x}$	`\dot{x}`	$\ddot{x}$	`\ddot{x}`

3.5.3 Brackets

$($	`(`	$)$	`)`	$\lceil$	`\lceil`	$\rceil$	`\rceil`
$[$	`[`	$]$	`]`	$\lfloor$	`\lfloor`	$\rfloor$	`\rfloor`
$\{$	`\{`	$\}$	`\}`	$\langle$	`\langle`	$\rangle$	`\rangle`
$\vert$	—	$\Vert$	\—				

Brackets can be set in various sizes or can be automatically adapted to the size of the respective expression to be enclosed. Naturally, the automatic adaptation variant is always preferable. The others are only mentioned here for the sake of completeness.

`(\frac{1}{2})`	$(\frac{1}{2})$
`\big(\frac{2}{3}\big)`	$\big(\frac{2}{3}\big)$
`\Big(\frac{3}{4}\Big)`	$\Big(\frac{3}{4}\Big)$
`\left(\frac{a+b}{\frac{a-b}{2}}\right)`	$\left(\frac{a+b}{\frac{a-b}{2}}\right)$

3.5.4 Commonly Used Symbols

$+$	`+`	$\oplus$	`\oplus`	$\vee$	`\vee`
$-$	`-`	$\ominus$	`\ominus`	$\wedge$	`\wedge`
$\cdot$	`\cdot`	$\odot$	`\odot`	$\cap$	`\cap`
$\div$	`\div`	$\oslash$	`\oslash`	$\cup$	`\cup`
$\times$	`\times`	$\otimes$	`\otimes`	$\uplus$	`\uplus`
$\circ$	`\circ`	$\bullet$	`\bullet`	$\bigcirc$	`\bigcirc`
∂	`\partial`	$\dagger$	`\dagger`	$\ddagger$	`\ddagger`
$\sum$	`\sum`	$\prod$	`\prod`	$\int$	`\int`
$\bigcap$	`\bigcap`	$\bigcup$	`\bigcup`	$\oint$	`\oint`
∇	`\nabla`				

3.5.5 Mathematical Functions

As mentioned above, the names of functions in a formula are typeset upright. To simplify this, corresponding commands are available for functions:

`\exp`	`\log`	`\ln`	`\lg`	`\sqrt`
`\sin`	`\cos`	`\tan`	`\sec`	`\cot`
`\arcsin`	`\arccos`	`\arctan`	`\deg`	`\hom`
`\sinh`	`\cosh`	`\tanh`	`\det`	`\dim`
`\lim`	`\limsup`	`\liminf`	`\arg`	`\gcd`
`\max`	`\min`	`\sup`	`\inf`	`\Pr`

3.5.6 Relations

$=$	`=`	$<$	`<`	$>$	`>`
$\leq$	`\leq`	$\geq$	`\geq`	$\equiv$	`\equiv`
$\sim$	`\sim`	$\simeq$	`\simeq`	$\approx$	`\approx`
$\subset$	`\subset`	$\supset$	`\supset`	$\cong$	`\cong`
$\subseteq$	`\subseteq`	$\supseteq$	`\supseteq`	$\doteq$	`\doteq`
$\propto$	`\propto`	$\parallel$	`\parallel`	$\perp$	`\perp`
$\in$	`\in`	$\ni$	`\ni`	$\notin$	`\notin`
$\not=$	`\not=`	$\not<$	`\not<`	$\not>$	`\not>`
$\not\leq$	`\not\leq`	$\not\geq$	`\not\geq`	$\not\equiv$	`\not\equiv`
$\not\sim$	`\not\sim`	$\not\simeq$	`\not\simeq`	$\not\approx$	`\not\approx`
$\not\subset$	`\not\subset`	$\not\supset$	`\not\supset`	$\not\cong$	`\not\cong`
$\not\subseteq$	`\not\subseteq`	$\not\supseteq$	`\not\supseteq`	$\not\doteq$	`\not\doteq`
$\not\propto$	`\not\propto`	$\not\parallel$	`\not\parallel`	$\not\perp$	`\not\perp`

3.5.7 Arrows

$\leftarrow$	`\leftarrow`	$\rightarrow$	`\rightarrow`
$\longleftarrow$	`\longleftarrow`	$\longrightarrow$	`\longrightarrow`
$\leftrightarrow$	`\leftrightarrow`	$\longleftrightarrow$	`\longleftrightarrow`
$\Leftarrow$	`\Leftarrow`	$\Rightarrow$	`\Rightarrow`
$\Longleftarrow$	`\Longleftarrow`	$\Longrightarrow$	`\Longrightarrow`
$\Leftrightarrow$	`\Leftrightarrow`	$\Longleftrightarrow$	`\Longleftrightarrow`
$\uparrow$	`\uparrow`	$\downarrow$	`\downarrow`
$\Uparrow$	`\Uparrow`	$\Downarrow$	`\Downarrow`
$\updownarrow$	`\updownarrow`	$\Updownarrow$	`\Updownarrow`

$\leftharpoonup$	`\leftharpoonup`	$\rightharpoonup$	`\rightharpoonup`
$\leftharpoondown$	`\leftharpoondown`	$\rightharpoondown$	`\rightharpoondown`
$\rightleftharpoons$	`\rightleftharpoons`	$\mapsto$	`\mapsto`
$\nearrow$	`\nearrow`	$\searrow$	`\searrow`
$\nwarrow$	`\nwarrow`	$\swarrow$	`\swarrow`
$\hookleftarrow$	`\hookleftarrow`	$\hookrightarrow$	`\hookrightarrow`

3.5.8 Further Symbols

$\forall$	`\forall`	$\exists$	`\exists`	$\emptyset$	`\emptyset`
$\hbar$	`\hbar`	$\triangle$	`\triangle`	∞	`\infty`
$\imath$	`\imath`	$\jmath$	`\jmath`	ℓ	`\ell`
$\Re$	`\Re`	$\Im$	`\Im`	$\wp$	`\wp`
$\diamondsuit$	`\diamondsuit`	$\heartsuit$	`\heartsuit`		
$\spadesuit$	`\spadesuit`	$\clubsuit$	`\clubsuit`		

Chapter 4

Lists and Tables

LaTeX allows for the creation of various types of lists. What they have in common is that each list item is preceded by the `\item` command.

4.1 Various List Types

For an unordered list, you use the `itemize` environment, which by default places a `\textbullet` • before each item.

```
\begin{itemize}
  \item first item
  \item second item
  \begin{itemize}
    \item sub-item 1
    \item sub-item 2
  \end{itemize}
  \item[$>>$] third item
\end{itemize}
```

list!itemize@*itemize*

- first item
- second item
  - sub-item 1
  - sub-item 2

$>>$ third item

To change the list symbol, you append the new symbol in square brackets to the `\item` command. To create a numbered list, we replace `itemize` with `enumerate`:

```
\begin{enumerate}
  \item first item
  \item second item
  \begin{itemize}
    \item sub-item 1
    \item sub-item 2
  \end{itemize}
  \item third item
\end{enumerate}
```

1. first item
2. second item
   - sub-item 1
   - sub-item 2
3. third item

As illustrated in both examples, lists can also be nested. During this process, the symbol or the type of numbering is changed respectively.

A list of terms with explanations can also be easily written using LaTeX :

```
\begin{description}
  \item[one:] explanation 1
  \item[two:] explanation 2
  \item[three:] explanation 3
\end{description}
```

one: explanation 1

two: explanation 2

three: explanation 3

4.2 Tables

Tables can be created using the `tabular` environment. The procedure is the same as for arrays, which were already introduced in the context of mathematical environments in Chapter 3. Here, too, the number of columns and the column alignment must be defined in curly brackets after opening the environment. As with the array, new columns are started with an & as a control character, while a double backslash \\ defines the end of a line. All of this is illustrated in the following example:

```
\begin{tabular}{l c r}
left & centre & right\\
l    & c      & r
\end{tabular}
```

left	centre	right
l	c	r

Additional column properties can also be defined within the brackets where the text alignment is specified. If you enter a vertical bar (or several) between two specifications, these will be adopted as column separators. An `\hline` after a line break creates a horizontal line:

```
\begin{tabular}{l|c|r}
left & centre & right\\\hline
l    & c      & r
\end{tabular}
```

left	centre	right
l	c	r

Using the format specification `p{x}`, you can achieve a fixed column width. The column is then typeset as justified text. In this context, `x` represents a length in the units that were already introduced in Chapter 2.

```
\begin{tabular}{l|p{2cm}}
left  & justified\\\hline
l     & column with a fixed width
\end{tabular}
```

left	justified
l	column with a fixed width

The text width `\textwidth` can be used as an additional unit. For instance, `p{0.6\textwidth}` creates a column that occupies 60% of the page width. Furthermore, LaTeX offers many other formatting options for tables, some of which will be briefly introduced here.

Special separators between two columns can be specified using `@{x}`, where `x` represents the chosen separator. If this expression is placed between two format specifications, the corresponding columns will always be separated by the specified symbol.

If you place the command

```
\multicolumn{number of columns}{format}{text}
```

into a table cell, you can override the global format specifications for that specific row and span a cell across multiple columns. During this process, all format specifications for this cell must be redefined.

The command `\cline{n-m}` draws a horizontal line after a table row in the specified columns, where `n` denotes the starting column and `m` the ending column. All of this will now be illustrated using the example of a timetable:

```
\begin{tabular}{|r@{ - }l||l|l|}
\hline
\multicolumn{2}{|l||}{Time} & Monday & Tuesday\\
\hline\hline
8  & 9  & Physics  & Maths   \\\cline{1-2}\cline{4-4}
9  & 10 &          & English\\\hline
10 & 11 & Maths    & \LaTeX  \\\hline
\end{tabular}
```

Time	Monday	Tuesday
8 - 9	Physics	Maths
9 - 10		English
10 - 11	Maths	LaTeX

Special float environments are available for tables, which also allow for the addition of table captions. These are explained in Chapter 5.

In the following, we will look at an example of a multi-page table. This requires the additional package `longtable`.

```
\begin{longtable}{|l|l|}

% Design for the first header
\hline
\textbf{Heading 1} & \textbf{Heading 2}\\
\hline
\endfirsthead


% Design of all other headers
\hline
\multicolumn{2}{|c|}{Table continuation}\\
\hline
\textbf{Heading 1} & \textbf{Heading 2}\\
\hline
\endhead


% Design of the footer
\hline
\multicolumn{2}{|c|}{Continued on the next page}\\
\hline
\endfoot


% Design of the last footer
\hline
\endlastfoot
```

```
% Table content
Table entries & Table entries\\
Table entries & Table entries\\
Table entries & Table entries\\
Table entries & Table entries\\
Table entries & Table entries\\
Table entries & Table entries\\
Table entries & Table entries\\
Table entries & Table entries\\
Table entries & Table entries\\
Table entries & Table entries\\
Table entries & Table entries\\
Table entries & Table entries\\
Table entries & Table entries\\
Table entries & Table entries\\
Table entries & Table entries\\
Table entries & Table entries\\
Table entries & Table entries
\end{longtable}
```

To improve the presentation of the table across multiple pages, the commands `\endhead`, `\endfirsthead`, `\endfoot`, and `\endlastfoot` are introduced. The table header and footer are separated from the content by `\endfirsthead` and `\endhead`, or `\endfoot` and `\endlastfoot` respectively. The result achieved with this source code is the following table:

Heading 1	**Heading 2**
Table entries	Table entries
Table entries	Table entries
Table entries	Table entries
Table entries	Table entries
Table entries	Table entries
Table entries	Table entries
Table entries	Table entries
Table entries	Table entries
Table entries	Table entries
Table entries	Table entries
Table entries	Table entries
Continued on the next page	

Table continuation	
Heading 1	**Heading 2**
Table entries	Table entries
Table entries	Table entries
Table entries	Table entries
Table entries	Table entries
Table entries	Table entries
Table entries	Table entries
Table entries	Table entries
Table entries	Table entries
Table entries	Table entries
Table entries	Table entries
Table entries	Table entries
Table entries	Table entries
Table entries	Table entries
Table entries	Table entries
Table entries	Table entries
Table entries	Table entries
Table entries	Table entries
Table entries	Table entries
Table entries	Table entries
Table entries	Table entries
Table entries	Table entries
Table entries	Table entries
Table entries	Table entries
Table entries	Table entries
Table entries	Table entries
Table entries	Table entries
Table entries	Table entries
Table entries	Table entries
Table entries	Table entries
Table entries	Table entries
Table entries	Table entries
Table entries	Table entries
Table entries	Table entries
Table entries	Table entries
Table entries	Table entries
Table entries	Table entries
Table entries	Table entries
Continued on the next page	

Table continuation	
Heading 1	**Heading 2**
Table entries	Table entries
Table entries	Table entries
Table entries	Table entries
Table entries	Table entries
Table entries	Table entries
Table entries	Table entries
Table entries	Table entries
Table entries	Table entries
Table entries	Table entries
Table entries	Table entries
Table entries	Table entries
Table entries	Table entries
Table entries	Table entries
Table entries	Table entries
Table entries	Table entries
Table entries	Table entries
Table entries	Table entries

Chapter 5

Graphics and Float Objects

Graphics and tables are essential elements of most scientific papers, especially in the fields of natural sciences and engineering. To clarify and explain many issues or to present results, they are simply indispensable.

5.1 Including Graphics

Once the `graphicx` package is loaded, various graphics formats can be included. With standard LaTeX (conversion to *DVI* or *Postscript*), only graphics in *Postscript* (*PS*) or *Encapsulated Postscript* (*EPS*) formats can be used, whereas with *PDF*-LaTeX (direct conversion to *PDF*), graphics files in *JPG*, *PNG*, or *PDF* can be employed. For all formats, the command `\includegraphics[options]{file}` is used. Available options include the image height (`height`), the width (`width`), and a rotation angle (`angle`). For width and height, all units of length (e.g. *pt*, *cm*, *mm*, or `\textwidth`) can be used. The angle is entered in degrees, with counter-clockwise rotation being positive.

```
\includegraphics[width=0.5\textwidth]{image1.png}
\includegraphics[height=3cm,angle=90]{image1.png}
```

Image sections can be displayed using the clip and viewport options:

```
\includegraphics[width=4cm]{image1.png}
\includegraphics[width=4cm,clip,
            viewport=20 200 380 300]{image1.png}
```

As shown in the example above, `viewport = k l m n` is entered as an option of the `includegraphics` command. The four numbers `k`, `l`, `m`, and `n` describe the left, bottom, right, and top edges of the image section, each specified as distances from the left (`k` and `m`) and bottom (`l` and `n`) edges, respectively.

5.2 Float Objects

Float objects serve, for example, as environments for graphics and tables, but can also contain many other things. They get their name from the property that their position in the typeset document is not determined solely by where they are found in the source code. Instead, LaTeX inserts them in such a way that the available space throughout the entire document is utilised optimally. However, this can sometimes lead to the author having an aesthetic preference that differs from the result, necessitating a tough battle with LaTeX until everything is truly well typeset.

We intend to describe the properties of such objects using the `figure` environment, which is typically used for figures. Tables, on the other hand, are enclosed in the `table` environment, which is handled in the same manner and possesses the same properties as the `figure` environment:

```
\begin{figure}[position]        \begin{table}[position]
...                             ...
\end{figure}                    \end{table}
```

For the position, you can choose between four different options:

t	top	Next available opportunity at the top of a page
b	bottom	Next available opportunity at the bottom of a page
h	here	At the same position as in the source code (if possible, otherwise at the next suitable position)
p	page	On a separate page containing only float objects (a so-called *float page*)

However, this selection does not guarantee the desired positioning with 100% certainty. If an environment simply does not fit at the requested position, LaTeX will independently choose a more suitable location. If you wish to increase the priority of your own preference, you can prefix the option with a `!`. Furthermore, it is possible to specify a selection of potential positions:

```
\begin{figure}[t]
\begin{figure}[!h]
\begin{figure}[tb]
```

A figure or table caption is obtained by using

```
\caption[short text]{caption text}
```

within the `figure` or `table` environment. Here, `caption text` represents the text that is placed directly above or below the graphic or table.

In contrast, `short text` is a placeholder for a brief summary or a short title of the figure, which will be found in the list of figures or list of tables for better clarity. If no lists of figures or tables are to be created, the short text can also be omitted (`\caption{caption text}`).

When a caption is created, a number is assigned to the figure or table, which can then be used for referencing in the text. To avoid having to do this manually, a label with a unique name must be assigned to the figure (or table) using the command `\label{labelname}` within the float environment after the caption. Duplicate names within a single source code are prohibited and will result in error messages and incorrect representations in the typeset document. This label can then be called at any point in the source code using `\ref{labelname}`.

An implementation in the source code could, for example, look like this:

```
\begin{figure}[!h]
\begin{center}
\includegraphics[width=\textwidth]{image2.png}
\caption[Short version]{Figure with caption.}
\label{label-example-2}
\end{center}
\end{figure}
```

Figure 5.1: Figure with caption.

Finally, the command `\ref{labelname}` can be used to refer to the image within the text:

```
Figure \ref{label-example-2}
shows a simple example of a
figure with a caption.
```

Figure 5.1 shows a simple example of a figure with a caption.

A small tip regarding figure and table captions: It is of great benefit to the reader if these stand out more visually from the rest of the text than they usually do with the standard settings. It is advisable to set captions with slightly larger margins and also to change the font. For example, set the captions in `\small` or in `\textit`. For a simplification of this process, please feel free to take a look at the `caption` package.

Just like a table of contents, lists of tables and lists of figures can be generated using the commands `\listoftables` and `\listoffigures`, respectively.

Chapter 6

Advanced Elements

In addition to the functions described so far, LaTeX offers a wealth of additional commands, packages, and document classes. Some of these will be briefly described here. In some cases, they are not found in standard LaTeX installations and must be added subsequently. Traditional internet search engines are a great help when searching for new commands and packages. Installation instructions for new packages can usually be found on the developers' respective websites or in an accompanying file.

As a brief outlook, some commands and structures will already be introduced at this point; although they go beyond an introductory course, they are very frequently used in practice.

6.1 Defining New Commands

Every user can define new commands in the header of the LaTeX source code, which can subsequently be used. In doing so, the properties and arguments of the new command must be specified:

```
\newcommand{command}[arguments][default]{definition}
```

First, the name of the desired command must be specified, starting with a \. However, it must not have been defined previously – meaning it cannot correspond to any command that either exists in the standard LaTeX set or has been loaded via an additional package. This is followed by the number of arguments (0–9) that must be passed to the command when it is used. Optionally, a default value can now be added; this is used in place of the first argument if it is not provided when using the command. Finally, the definition of the new command is required, where the command's arguments can be called using #1 to #9.

Here is a small example intended to clarify the use of \newcommand:

```
\newcommand{\myangle}[2]{<\!\!\!)\,\left(#1,#2\right)}
```

The newly created \myangle command has two arguments and must be used in the form:

```
\verb|\myangle{argument1}{argument2}|
```

The curly brackets

```
\verb|{<\!\!\!)\,\left(#1,#2\right)}|
```

describe how LaTeX should handle these arguments. Once this command is defined in the header of the source code, it can be used subsequently at any point. Due to its structure as a mathematical symbol, however, it must be placed within a mathematical environment:

```
$\myangle{\vec{a}}{\vec{b}}$
```

$\sphericalangle\left(\vec{a},\vec{b}\right)$

Naturally, it is also possible to define a command without any arguments:

```
\newcommand{\myanglesym}{<\!\!\!)}
```

and finally use it within the source code:

```
$\myanglesym$
```

$\sphericalangle$

To replace an existing command, \renewcommand can be used. In contrast, \providecommand is only executed if the command defined by it is not yet known. Both have the same options and properties as the basic \newcommand.

6.2 The input Command

For longer documents or projects with many authors, it can be useful to split the content into various source files, which can later be merged into one. A part of the source code can simply be outsourced and reintegrated using the command `\input{filename}`. In this way, for example, form and content can be separated:

```
\documentclass[a4paper,12pt]{article}
\usepackage[utf8]{inputenc}
\usepackage[english]{babel}

\begin{document}
\maketitle
\tableofcontents

\input{content/chapter_01.inc}
\input{content/chapter_02.inc}
\input{content/chapter_03.inc}
\input{content/chapter_04.inc}
\input{content/chapter_05.inc}
\input{content/chapter_06.inc}

\end{document}
```

6.3 Cross-References

The commands `\label{labelname}` and `\ref{labelname}`, already familiar from Chapter 5, can be used for more than just referencing figures and tables. Labels can be placed at any desired location within the source code. `\ref{labelname}` then refers to the corresponding chapter, section, or even formula number, while `\pageref{labelname}` indicates the page on which the referenced label is located.

At this point, it should once again be noted that label names must be unique within a document and must not occur more than once.

6.4 Appendices

In principle, appendices are written in the same way as the rest of the document. The same structure is maintained; however, there is a switch from naming chapters to naming appendices. The appendices are introduced with the command `\appendix`. In the document classes book or `report`, each individual appendix is a `chapter`. The numbering changes from numbers (Chapter 1, 2, 3...) to capital letters (Appendix A, B, C...).

```
\chapter{Data Evaluation and Comparison with
         Model Calculations}
...

\chapter{Summary and Outlook}
...

\appendix

\chapter{Mathematical Fundamentals}
...

\chapter{Numerical Implementation}
...

\chapter{Estimation of Numerical Errors}
...
```

Chapter 7

Bibliographies and Citations with BibTEX

In almost all academic papers, it is necessary to create a bibliography and work with citations. In doing so, one ideally wants to be able to conveniently access a (self-created) database containing all the essential information regarding the cited sources. From this, one aims to generate consistently formatted citations quickly and easily, which are then used to automatically produce a bibliography with uniform formatting, including all the sources referenced.

All of this is possible with LaTeX. *BibTeX* offers the possibility to create a bibliographic database and integrate it into a LaTeX document. This database can be accessed using commands to cite sources in various ways. It is also possible to choose between different citation and bibliography styles, which differ in the arrangement of the literature in the bibliography and the structure of the citations.

Attention: Citation culture varies across different academic disciplines. Inquire early on about what is expected of you.

First, an additional text file is created, which should be located in the same directory as the LaTeX document. This file is saved with the extension *.bib* (for bibliography), e.g. *literature.bib*. The bibliographic database created in this way, which is initially empty, is integrated into the LaTeX document at the desired location using the command

```
\bibliography{filename without extension}
```

which, in our example, would be

```
\bibliography{literature}
```

With the integration of the bibliography, the number of compilation runs required increases. To generate the bibliography and citations correctly, LATEX requires an additional processing step beyond the two runs needed for an error-free table of contents. In most LATEX editors, *BibTeX* is executed automatically. If this is not the case for you, you should consult the manual or the help section of your editor.

7.1 Creating a Bibliographic Database

Now we are ready to fill the bibliographic database. For this purpose, entries of the following form are used:

```
@article{identifier,
  author = {Surname1, Firstname1 and Surname2,
           Firstname2 and ...},
  title = {Title of the article},
  journal = {Name of the journam,
  volume = {Volume},
  number = {Number},
  pages = {First page -- last page},
  year = {Year in XXXX},
  month = {Month}
}
```

The format of the cited entry (articles, books, PhD theses, manuals, etc.) follows the @ symbol. An overview of the various formats is shown in Table 7.1. Immediately following the first curly bracket is a unique identifier, similar to the label command, which is used in the LATEX source code to access the corresponding entry in the bibliographic database. This is followed by the data required for the entry (authors, title, year of publication, journal, publisher, etc.). Table 7.1 lists which details are mandatory or optional for different types of literature.

It is usually not necessary to create the entries for the bibliographic database manually. For most academic disciplines, online databases can be found from which the corresponding entries in *BibTeX* format can be retrieved. In the fields of astronomy and space physics, for example, this is NASA's ADS (Astrophysics Data System). Similar systems exist for other areas or are even interdisciplinary. There, one can find and download specialist literature on many topics via a search query.

Reference	Mandatory fields	Optional fields
article	author, title, journal, year	volume, number, pages, month, note
book	author oder editor, title, publisher, year	volume oder number, series, address, edition, month, note, isbn
booklet	title	author, howpublished, address, month, year, note
conference	author, title, booktitle, year	editor, volume oder number, series, pages, address, month, organisation, publisher, note
inbook	author oder editor, title, chapter und/oder pages, publisher, year	volume oder number, series, type, address, edition, month, note
incollection	author, title, booktitle, publisher, year	editor, volume oder number, series, type, chapter, pages, address, edition, month, note
inproceedings	author, title, booktitle, year	editor, volume oder number, series, pages, address, month, organisation, publisher, note
manual	title	author, organisation, address, edition, month, year, note
mastersthesis	author, title, school, year	type, address, month, note
misc	—	author, title, howpublished, month, year, note
phdthesis	author, title, school, year	type, address, month, note
proceedings	title, year	editor, volume oder number, series, address, month, organisation, publisher, note
techreport	author, title, institution, year	type, number, address, month, note
unpublished	author, title, note	month, year

Table 7.1: Various document formats and their mandatory and optional fields.

Furthermore, these systems also provide the *BibTeX* entries belonging to the respective literature, including all the essential information.

If you wish to cite a book, search engines can be used to find websites that offer a service to generate *BibTeX* entries for specific books from the catalogues of major online retailers.

In a short example, we create *BibTeX* entries for an article and a book:

```
@article{Jok1995,
  author = {{Jokipii}, J.~R. and {K{\'o}ta}, J.
          and {Giacalone}, J. and {Horbury}, T.~S.
      and {Smith}, E.~J.},
  title = {Interpretation and consequences of
         large-scale magnetic variances observed
             at high heliographic latitude},
  journal = {Geophysical Research Letters},
  year = 1995,
  volume = 22,
  pages = {3385-3388}
}

@book{BaumTreu2022,
  author = {Baumjohann, Wolfgang and
           Treumann, Rudolf A.},
  title = {{Basic Space Plasma Physics}},
  publisher = {{WSPC}},
  edition = {3rd},
  isbn = {9811254400},
  year = {2022},
  month = {feb}
}
```

7.2 Bibliography Styles and Citations

The structure of the bibliography and the appearance of citations within the text depend on the selected bibliography style. *BibTeX* includes many options, some of which will be briefly introduced here. First, however, the package `natbib` is recommended to the interested LATEX user, as it achieves significantly better results than the default settings. As a simple example, let us first look at the `plain` style:

```
\bibliography{literature}
\bibliographystyle{plain}
```

In the source code, you can now access the bibliographic database using the commands `\cite`, `\citet`, and `\citep`. All sources cited in this way are automatically added to the bibliography. In the case of the `plain` style, this will appear as a chapter titled "Bibliography" when using the `book` or `report` classes. For all other document classes, a new section titled "References" will be created.

[1] J. R. Jokipii, J. Kóta, J. Giacalone, T. S. Horbury, and E. J. Smith. Interpretation and consequences of large-scale magnetic variances observed at high heliographic latitude. *Geophysical Research Letters*, 22:3385-3388, 1995.

[2] Wolfgang Baumjohann, Rudolf A. Treumann. *Basic Space Plasma Physics* WSPC, 3rd Ed., Feb. 2022.

In Table 7.2, the use of the various `\cite` commands is demonstrated using the example of the bibliographic database created above; note that there are no differences between these commands when using `plain` as the bibliography style.

If you wish to add sources from the database to the bibliography without citing them in the text, the command `\nocite{identifier}` can be used. By using `\nocite{*}`, all entries from the database are included in the bibliography.

As a further example of bibliography styles, we use `plainnat` from the `natbib` package:

```
\bibliography{literature}
\bibliographystyle{plainnat}
```

Command	**Representation in the text**
`\cite{BaumTreu2022}`	[2]
`\citep{Jok1995}`	[1]
`\citet{BaumTreu2022}`	[2]
`\citep[siehe z.B.][]{Jok1995}`	[siehe z.B. 1]
`\citet[siehe z.B.][]{Jok1995}`	[siehe z.B. 1]
`\citep[siehe z.B.][u.a.]{Jok1995,BaumTreu2022}`	[siehe z.B. 1, 2 u.a.]
`\citet[siehe z.B.][u.a.]{Jok1995,BaumTreu2022}`	[siehe z.B. 1, 2 u.a.]

Table 7.2: Output formats of various citation commands using the *plain* bibliography style as an example.

Command	Representation in the text
\cite{BaumTreu2022}	Baumjohann and Treumann [2022]
\citep{Jok1995}	[Jokipii et al., 1995]
\citet{BaumTreu2022}	Baumjohann and Treumann [2022]
\citep[z.B.][]{Jok1995}	[z.B. Jokipii et al., 1995]
\citet[z.B.][]{Jok1995}	Jokipii et al. [z.B. 1995]

Table 7.3: Output formats of various citation commands using the *plainnat* bibliography style from the *natbib* package as an example.

The presentation of the bibliography is slightly modified:

J. R. Jokipii, J. Kóta, J. Giacalone, T. S. Horbury, and E. J. Smith. Interpretation and consequences of large-scale magnetic variances observed at high heliographic latitude. *Geophysical Research Letters*, 22:3385-3388, 1995.
Wolfgang Baumjohann, Rudolf A. Treumann. *Basic Space Plasma Physics* WSPC, 3rd Ed., Feb. 2022. ISBN 9811254400.

Even though the commands for the citations are the same in all bibliography styles, the representation of the citations in the text with `plainnat` differs significantly from the `plain` style. This is demonstrated in Table 7.3.
The use of `elsart-harv`:

```
\bibliography{literature}
\bibliographystyle{elsart-harv}
```

leads to several further changes, both in the bibliography:

J. R. Jokipii, J. Kóta, J. Giacalone, T. S. Horbury, and E. J. Smith, 1995. Interpretation and consequences of large-scale magnetic variances observed at high heliographic latitude. Geophysical Research Letters 22, 3385-3388.
Wolfgang Baumjohann, Rudolf A. Treumann, Feb. 2022. Basic Space Plasma Physics, 3rd edition. WSPC.

and in the citations (see Table 7.4).

Command	**Representation in the text**
`\cite{BaumTreu2022}`	Baumjohann and Treumann (2022)
`\citep{Jok1995}`	(Jokipii et al., 1995)
`\citet{BaumTreu2022}`	Baumjohann and Treumann (2022)
`\citep[z.B.]{Jok1995}`	(z.B. Jokipii et al., 1995)
`\citet[z.B.]{Jok1995}`	Jokipii et al. (z.B. 1995)

Table 7.4: Output formats of various citation commands using the *elsart-harv* bibliography style as an example.

There is a vast number of bibliography styles available. Their names can be found in the *BibTeX* directory. To find out exactly which style you want (or even need) to use, you should simply try out a few of them.

Chapter 8

Bibliographies and Citations with BibLaTeX

While BibTeX (see Chapter 7) represents the traditional method in the LaTeX world, BibLaTeX has established itself as a modern and more powerful tool. This chapter introduces the use of BibLaTeX and demonstrates how to set it up in common editors.

8.1 Configuration and Usage of the Biber Backend

Since BibLaTeX requires the *Biber* backend program, the compilation process in your editor must be adjusted. Instead of the traditional chain LaTeX → BibTeX → LaTeX → LaTeX, the chain **LaTeX** → **Biber** → **LaTeX** → **LaTeX** is used.

The exact settings for the compilation profiles can be found on relevant websites. AI systems also generally provide good guidance. Table 8.1 provides an initial overview.

8.2 Integrating BibLaTeX

In contrast to BibTeX, BibLaTeX must be loaded and configured as a package in the preamble (header):

Editor	Adjustment (Compilation Profile)
TeXnicCenter	Create a new compilation profile or edit an existing one (e.g. LaTeX → PDF). The *Biber call* is inserted between the first and second LaTeX runs: LaTeX → Biber → LaTeX → LaTeX.
TeXworks	Define a new tool in the *preferences menu* that calls *Biber* and adjust the workflow chain.
VS Code with LaTeX Workshop	In most cases, the modern LaTeX Workshop extension automatically detects the `biblatex` package and the required `biber` backend. In this case, no manual adjustment is necessary.

Table 8.1: Adjustment of the compilation profile in various editors.

```
% In the document header (preamble):
\usepackage[
    backend=biber,       % Selects the modern backend
    style=authoryear,    % Defines the citation style
    sorting=nyvt         % Defines the sorting
]{biblatex}
\addbibresource{literatur.bib} % Includes the .bib
                               % file (with
                               % extension!)
```

- `backend=biber`: Ensures that the modern Biber program is used.
- `style=...`: Defines the appearance of citations and the bibliography.
- `sorting=...`: Defines the type of sorting used in the bibliography.
- `\addbibresource{...}`: Replaces `\bibliography`. The bibliography file must be specified with its extension.

The `style` option can be used to influence the appearance of citations and the bibliography. The most commonly used options are `authoryear` and `numeric`.

Option	Explanation
`numeric`	This style is frequently used in shorter academic publications, e.g. in conference proceedings. It produces numerical citations following the pattern *[1]* or *[1, 2]*, which refer to the position in the bibliography.
`authoryear`	A style used in many natural science or engineering papers, which cites with the names of the authors and the year of publication, e.g. Feynman (1948), (Feynman, 1948) or Cook et al. (2013).
`verbose`	This style is more commonly used in the humanities. It is similar to the `authoryear` style, but provides the full information upon the first citation and uses a short version from the second citation onwards.

8.3 Creating a Literature Database

The `.bib` file is created in the same format as for BibTEX(see Chapter 7), since BibLATEX uses the same fields (`author`, `title`, `year` etc.) and reference types (`@article`, `@book`, `@phdthesis` etc.). The flexibility of BibLATEX lies in its processing.

We use the same entries in the following examples as in Chapter 7:

```
@article{Jok1995,
  author = {{Jokipii}, J.~R. and {K{\'o}ta}, J.
          and {Giacalone}, J. and {Horbury}, T.~S.
      and {Smith}, E.~J.},
  title = {Interpretation and consequences of
         large-scale magnetic variances observed
            at high heliographic latitude},
  journal = {Geophysical Research Letters},
  year = 1995,
  volume = 22,
  pages = {3385-3388}
}
```

```
@book{BaumTreu2022,
  author = {Baumjohann, Wolfgang and
           Treumann, Rudolf A.},
  title = {{Basic Space Plasma Physics}},
  publisher = {{WSPC}},
  edition = {3rd},
  isbn = {9811254400},
  year = {2022},
  month = {feb}
}
```

8.4 Citation Commands and Output

BibLaTeX offers a variety of citation commands that allow for precise control over how the citation appears in the text, regardless of the chosen style. Here, we use the style defined in the preamble: `style=authoryear`.

Command	**Representation in the text**
`\parencite{Jokipii1995}`	(Jokipii et al. 1995)
`\textcite{Jokipii1995}`	Jokipii et al. (1995)
`\cite{Jokipii1995}`	Jokipii et al. 1995
`\citeauthor{Jokipii1995}`	Jokipii et al.
`\citeyear{Jokipii1995}`	1995

Table 8.2: Citation commands for BibLaTeX with the option *style=authoryear*.

BibLaTeX commands support two optional arguments, which are used to specify pages or notes (postfix and prefix):

Command: `\textcite[page 3386]{Jokipii1995}`
Output: Jokipii et al. (1995, page 3386)

Command: `\parencite[see][p. 3386]{Jokipii1995}`
Output: (see Jokipii et al. 1995, p. 3386)

8.5 Creating the Bibliography

The bibliography is generated within the document using the command `\printbibliography`. This is inserted at the exact location where the bibliography should be typeset in the document.

The appearance of the bibliography is completely controlled by the style chosen in the preamble. The following example shows the bibliography output with the option `style=authoryear`:

> **Jokipii, J. R., J. Kóta, J. Giacalone, T. S. Horbury und E. J. Smith** (1995). Interpretation and consequences of large-scale magnetic variances observed at high heliographic latitude. In: *Geophysical Research Letters* 22, S. 3385–3388.
> **Wolfgang Baumjohann, Rudolf A. Treumann** (2022). *Basic Space Plasma Physics* 3rd Ed. WSPC.

8.6 Citing Without Direct Output

BibLaTeX also allows for the generation of entries in the bibliography without a citation appearing in the text:

- `\nocite{label}`: Adds an entry to the bibliography even if it has not been explicitly cited in the text.
- `\nocite{*}`: Adds all entries from the `.bib` file to the bibliography.

8.7 Creating a Document with Multiple Bibliographies

BibLaTeX offers the possibility to provide different sections of a document (e.g. each chapter of a book) with their own bibliographies.

To create two or more separate bibliographies within a single document, the document is divided into appropriate sections. This can be done either via the `refsection` option of the `biblatex` package or manually by setting up `refsections`. Each `refsection` only collects the citations that occur within its environment.

8.7.1 Setup in the Preamble

When creating a document with more than one bibliography, the BibLATEX environment must be loaded with the `refsection` option. This offers various possibilities:

Option	Explanation
`refsection=none`	Manual division of refsections.
`refsection=chapter`	Each chapter is a `refsection` and each chapter receives its own bibliography via the `\printbibliography` command.
`refsection=section`	Each section is a `refsection` and each section receives its own bibliography via the `\printbibliography` command.

To prevent each of these bibliographies from becoming a separate chapter, the `\printbibliography` command is used in this case with the `heading=subbibliography` option:

```
\printbibliography[heading=subbibliography]
```

8.7.2 Example of Manual Division

```
...

\usepackage[backend=biber, style=authoryear,
            refsection=none]{biblatex}


...

\begin{document}

% First refsection
\begin{refsection}
  \section{Heading 1}
 Text with citations
 ...
 \section{Heading 2}
 Text with citations
 ...
 \section{Heading 3}
 Text with citations
```

```
 ...
  \printbibliography[heading=subbibliography]
\end{refsection}

...

% Second refsection
\begin{refsection}
  \section{Heading 4}
 Text with citations
 ...
 \section{Heading 5}
 Text with citations
 ...
  \printbibliography[heading=subbibliography]
\end{refsection}

...

\end{document}
```

Chapter 9

Academic Writing

At this point, we should take the time and the space to reflect on what we are doing here and why: we are learning LaTeX – a scripting language that is particularly well-suited for composing academic texts, especially in the mathematics-heavy fields of natural sciences and engineering. This very task – writing an academic text – is one that often accompanies us in the sciences from the beginning of our studies to the end of our careers: we write reports and protocols for internships and experiments, minutes of meetings, or summaries and handouts for seminar presentations and project work. Later, we write our theses, dissertations, and ultimately scientific contributions to conferences and academic journals.

It is precisely this extensive topic that we wish to address in this chapter. Naturally, it is far too broad to be treated briefly; indeed, it fills entire books by other authors. Nevertheless, the most important basic rules that every author of an academic paper should know can be summarised in just a few pages.

9.1 What is the Purpose of Academic Papers?

Writing an academic paper, regardless of the career stage at which it occurs, is one of the essential skills that should be acquired by the end of a degree. Through the numerous protocols and assignments we write during our studies, we practise for our final theses and, ultimately, for a potential academic career. With every academic paper we write, we aim to demonstrate our ability to work scientifically. In doing so, we advance the body of knowledge within our respective fields and propel our own careers forward.

As previously indicated, an academic text does not merely serve to document a gain in knowledge. Regardless of how remarkable your research findings may be, if you cannot present them in a positive, engaging manner using methods that meet established scientific standards, your work will be torn apart by reviewers or, at the latest, by your readers. Therefore, here are a few basic rules that you should observe in any case:

1. A good academic paper begins with thorough preparation. Document each step of your work in detail during your research. This ensures that you will always know exactly how your findings were obtained, allowing you to explain your methodologies and results to your readers clearly and comprehensively.

2. In a good academic paper, you address a clear research question and resolve it using established methods. If you use previously unknown methods, you must establish them yourself; that is, test them extensively and fully to prove their validity to your readers.

3. In a good academic paper, you do not merely present your own research findings; you also interpret them, scrutinise them critically, and compare them with the work and results of other scientists.

4. Above all, a good academic paper is written independently. Even though the temptation to copy from other scientists or perhaps even hire a ghostwriter or let AI do the work for you may be great, the many prominent examples of those who have stumbled over plagiarism scandals should serve as a cautionary tale and encourage you to always compose your work yourself.

9.2 Tips for the Preparation Phase

The final appearance of an academic paper depends on a great many factors, which you should clarify during the preparation phase.

First and foremost is the target audience. Who will read your paper? Students? Reviewers? Other scientists? Perhaps it will even be a popular science paper? What do you want to convey to this audience, and what objective are you pursuing yourself? The answers to these questions determine the academic depth you must or may achieve in your report. Are you only permitted to scratch the surface and required to use simple, figurative language? Or do you have to delve into the details of your research using technical scientific terminology and mathematical methods? Where do you intend to publish your research findings? And in which language? Are you writing alone or together with colleagues?

Once you have answered these questions – and likely many more – you can begin the next phase of your preparation:

9.2.1 Collecting and Selecting Content

There are many sources of information that you can draw upon for your academic reports and papers:

- Your own work: self-generated data, figures, calculations, derivations, and theories.
- Academic textbooks, specialist journals, and journal articles. All three options are available to you both online and offline.
- Other scientists (!)

If you are still completing your degree, specialists and textbooks in particular will be among your most important sources of information. You should not hesitate to visit your lecturers during their office hours to ask questions. If, for example, you are conducting an experiment during a practical course, record all the information and data you will need for the preparation of your report. Whenever possible, request any missing information directly from the supervisors of your experiments.

A particular note regarding online sources: in principle, you must, of course, verify the trustworthiness of each of your information sources. This is easier in some cases than in others. Books and specialist articles from established publishing houses, which usually must undergo a rigorous peer-review process before publication, can generally be used as sources without concern. However, this is not the case for many internet sources. Even Wikipedia articles can sometimes contain hair-raising errors!

9.2.2 Researching the Framework Conditions

The composition of an academic paper or a final thesis can be tied to a wide range of framework conditions. These may include, for example:

- time constraints and submission deadlines,
- formatting templates,
- minimum or maximum page counts,
- the language (e.g. English or German, but also technical versus easily understandable language), or
- certain preferences of your readers (e.g. those of your reviewers).

Once you have gathered all the essential information and content for your academic paper or final thesis, you can begin the writing phase. In practice, however, the preparation and writing phases are usually not clearly separable; instead, they alternate or even run parallel to one another.

9.3 Tips for the Writing Phase

We have already established that the composition of academic papers does not serve the sole purpose of documentation. Beyond this, it serves to strengthen one's own understanding, to critically engage with one's own work and that of others, and, of course, to present one's own findings. In this regard, it has little to nothing to do with the work of fiction writers or novelists. Since it follows strict rules, it more closely resembles the application of mathematics.

Academic writing does not need to create suspense and must never surprise the reader. Precise and unambiguous statements must be formulated, and clearly defined terms must be used. The language employed must be clear and comprehensible. Use appropriate terminology and technical language; colloquialisms are forbidden in academic papers. And it always applies: pay close attention to spelling, punctuation, and grammar. Use complete sentences.

9.3.1 Structure of an Academic Paper or Thesis

An academic paper has a standardised structure and can (but does not necessarily have to) include the following parts:

Title Page

Title pages are particularly common for final theses. They must contain all essential information regarding the work: title, author's name, date of publication or submission, university, and the department in which the thesis was written. Ensure you enquire which specific information must be included and which formatting guidelines you are required to follow.

Abstract
An abstract is a summary of the most important statements of the entire work, typically only a few lines long. It precedes the paper or thesis and is intended to help the reader decide whether the following text is of interest to them.

Table of Contents
A table of contents is usually only included in final theses and books. In (short) academic articles, it is generally not found at all.

Introduction
The introduction must provide a motivating entry into the topic of the following text. The research questions addressed in the report or thesis, as well as their academic relevance, must be highlighted clearly and comprehensibly. Frequently, the structure of the work is presented here, including brief summaries of the chapters. A summary of the key research findings presented in the work can also be useful at this stage.

Main Body
In the main body, the fundamentals and theoretical background (relevant to the work!) are explained first. The current state of research should be outlined as a starting point for your own research. This is followed by your own working methods (e.g. the setup and execution of an experiment or the explanation of a simulation code) and a detailed description of your own work (e.g. measurement or simulation results). Where possible, present data graphically. At the end of each main section, your results should be interpreted and critically evaluated. If possible, compare your results with those of other scientists. Address the question: what relevance do your research findings have for your field of study?

Summary
In the summary, you provide your readers with a concise overview of the most important results of your work. You also summarise

the critical engagement with your findings and the placement of your work within a broader context (relevance to the field of research). Often, an outlook on unresolved or newly emerged questions and future research objectives is also provided here.

Outlook
Particularly in longer academic papers and final theses, there may be a separate chapter on unresolved or newly emerged scientific questions and future research goals that build upon the results of your own research.

Lists and Appendices
Every academic paper must include a bibliography! It contains a complete list of all sources used during the creation of your work (literature and personal communication with "real" people). You can find more on this in Chapters 7 and 8. Furthermore, lists of figures or glossaries can also be part of an academic work, though these are typically only found in books or longer theses.

You can probably guess which parts are mandatory: the introduction, the main body, and the summary.

If you read the descriptions of the individual components of an academic paper carefully, you will quickly notice that the explanation of your work's central results, in particular, appears in many different places. This is not a selection of possible locations, but rather an obligation to repeat. As the author of an academic work, you must not – and indeed, are not permitted to – build suspense. The abstract, the summary, and the introduction are (in that order) the parts most frequently read by potential readers. Therefore, the most important results of your work must be summarised completely, comprehensibly, and in a motivating manner in each of these different sections.

Top-Down Approach to Writing

In principle, there are of course no strict regulations on exactly how you should proceed when writing an academic paper. However, in practice, a top-down approach in five stages has proved to be both sensible and helpful:

1. Creating a Macro Structure (Outline)
Create meaningful titles for all chapters (for longer papers and theses) or for individual sections (for shorter reports). Following

this, determine (equally clear) titles for the sub-chapters and check the structure for consistency and a "common thread". If you are writing a final thesis, have this structure reviewed by your examiner or reviewer.

2. **Structural Revision**
   If necessary, revise the structure of your outline and check it again. Repeat this step until all parties involved are satisfied.

3. **Developing and Filling the Microstructure**
   Formulate exactly one core statement for each section of your work. Then, populate the sections with bullet points. Subsequently, expand your text using these core statements and bullet points. Important: do not lose sight of the "common thread" while writing. Your text must be inherently consistent!

4. **Self-Correction**
   Read through your work exactly once yourself and check your statements for logic, consistency, and accuracy. A spell check certainly wouldn't go amiss either. Incorporate your own corrections into the work. Further self-corrections are often not useful, as authors tend to develop a certain "blinkeredness" relatively quickly.

5. **External Correction**
   Give your work to two or three other selected individuals to read and insist on rigorous corrections. They often spot more errors than you do yourself and can check your texts for clarity. At least one of these proofreaders should be capable of understanding your work from a technical perspective. A proofreader who pays particular attention to language and spelling should also be part of your team. Evaluate the suggested corrections for logic, relevance, and accuracy. Never incorporate suggestions blindly into your work.

Congratulations! Your work is done.

Maintaining Focus

As a general rule, an academic report should address exactly one research question. Should you, in exceptional cases, deal with more than one question within a single report, the structure of the document must be very clearly adapted. Define the scope of your work precisely. Which topics are addressed, and which might even be intentionally excluded, and why? Provide clear justifications for your choices!

Never Surprise the Reader

In academic papers, it is never a good idea to burden the reader with suspense or unexpected plot twists. Concentrate on the essentials.

If you are writing a longer piece of work, such as a thesis or a dissertation, you should briefly explain and summarise the structure and content of each subsequent chapter at its beginning. In this way, you ensure that your readers can quickly orientate themselves at any point in your work. Cross-references (see Chapter 6) are also a very helpful means of providing your readers with better guidance.

Consistency and Unambiguously Defined Terms

Naturally, your work must be self-contained and internally consistent. In this regard, it is helpful, among other things, to use only unambiguously defined terms and abbreviations and – should these not be universally applicable or well-known – to explain them yourself upon their first mention.

Even if you likely learnt in English lessons that varied language and an extensive vocabulary are marks of great style, the exact opposite applies to academic texts. You are not writing a novel. Do not confuse your readers by using numerous synonyms for the same term; with every synonym, your readers are forced to consider whether this newly introduced term might, in the context of your work, have a slightly modified or even entirely different meaning.

Evidence and Substantiation

It cannot be stressed often enough: in an academic paper, every statement must be clearly substantiated. In principle, you have two ways of doing this:

1. You can substantiate a statement with a literature citation and refer to the original author of that statement. However, you are more than welcome to replace the word "can" with the word "must", because whenever you are not the originator of a statement, that statement comes from someone else. In academia, the following

principle applies: credit where credit is due. Do not rest on someone else's laurels; otherwise, your work can quickly become an act of plagiarism.

2. Naturally, you do not need to substantiate your own statements, for which you are the originator, with external citations. However, your own statements always require sound reasoning or a line of argument. It is essential to demonstrate that your statements correspond to the truth and are not merely fabricated. This is what distinguishes credible and trustworthy scientists from people who argue with unprovable "alternative facts".

A notable exception is generally known facts. No one would dream of citing Isaac Newton's "Philosophiae Naturalis Principia Mathematica" (1687) when using $F = ma$.

When you use citations (see Chapters 7 and 8), always cite primary sources. Nothing is more frustrating for a reader than being forced to work their way through a pile of secondary literature[1]. Therefore, you must ensure that statements you cite can actually be found in the corresponding cited articles. Furthermore, in most academic disciplines, Wikipedia and trivial literature are not considered trustworthy sources.

Furthermore, for every academic paper (with the exception of textbooks, reviews, and other survey articles), a significant original contribution must be evident. How large this contribution should be often depends on the specific field in which the work is written and the academic level of the author. The further you progress in your studies or career, the more original work is expected of you.

Using Figures and Tables Effectively

To use a well-worn cliché: a picture is worth a thousand words. This is particularly true for the scientific presentation of data and relationships in figures. Therefore, it is essential to ensure a clear design for your figures, as well as correct axis labels and table headings. Use only colours and line types that are easily distinguishable. (A small tip for theses or

[1] A brief anecdote from my academic life: I once read an article that cited a fact I wanted to use for my dissertation. So, I read the cited article as well, only to find that the fact in question was not presented there as an original finding, but was merely cited again. I had to work my way through a series of articles, only to discover in the end that the fact I was looking for was not mentioned at all in the paper finally identified as the primary source. Although most of the articles I had to read during my research were more or less interesting, I felt rather... well, let us leave it at that.

dissertations: enquire whether any of your examiners or supervisors are colour-blind.)

Briefly explain figures and tables in captions (see Chapter 5). In the "normal" text, you can follow up with comprehensive descriptions and explanations. In doing so, however, ensure that you include a reference to the object being explained.

Note: If you use figures originating from external sources, it is often necessary to obtain written permission from the publisher and/or the author.

Plagiarism

In the German media, the term "plagiarism" has appeared with increasing frequency in recent years. In several prominent cases, the focus was on the revocation of doctoral degrees. Although a relevant violation could not always be established, the public, as well as universities and examination offices, have become more vigilant. This heightened attention now extends even to "lesser" pieces of work.

In the digital age, however, monitoring is much easier than in former times. Many institutes are now equipped with appropriate screening software to quickly and conveniently prove plagiarism in cases of suspicion. Therefore, a word of urgent advice at this point: even on a small scale and in the very early stages of a degree (e.g. in laboratory reports), plagiarism can lead to the failure of examinations and, in the worst-case scenario, to expulsion from the university.

9.4 General Tips for Daily Work

A degree programme is difficult to plan. Even if you start with the conviction that you will have your Bachelor's degree in the bag after three years and leave university with a Master's after a further two, a great deal can happen during those five years. Academic work is even less predictable, as it always involves exploring something completely unknown and does not follow a clearly predefined path. In this regard, only discipline, self-reflection, and self-management can help.

Here, too, there are a few clichés that are easily shared: do not put off unpleasant tasks. Do not take on too much at once; instead, break down extensive tasks into manageable steps and set yourself realistic deadlines. Sometimes social pressure also helps. Meet regularly with others (e.g. fellow students or colleagues) to exchange updates on the progress of your work. But remember: despite all the self-optimisation[2], procrastination can also be a bloody good and important thing. As long as you do not overdo it!

However, no matter how much effort you put into writing an academic paper, ultimately, the quality of such work cannot always be assessed entirely objectively. Naturally, there are objective criteria, which are applied particularly in peer-review processes prior to the publication of an academic article: the quality of the underlying data, the relevance of the statements made, the evidence and its implications, the clarity of the article, and, of course, whether a piece of work has been written according to strict academic rules.

However, particularly in the assessment of theses and dissertations, there are also many subjective criteria that may not be apparent to outsiders: how did the work come about? Did the author work independently? Or was a great deal of support from supervisors and colleagues required? Was the collaboration within the team always seamless?

A great many different criteria therefore influence the assessment of a piece of work; these are not always weighted equally, and some are beyond your control. Consequently, as an author, you have only one important goal, and that is satisfaction. You must satisfy yourself as well as your examiners or supervisors. If your work is published, then your readers naturally also belong to this select group. What you do not need to strive for, however, is perfectionism.

[2]One of my professors once said: "One of the most important tasks of a scientist is to occasionally sit by the window in peace and simply look out." He was right!

Chapter 10

Designing Presentations with LaTeX

LaTeX Beamer is a very user-friendly package for creating presentations. In contrast to standard commercial software, it dispenses with superfluous and distracting gimmicks, focusing instead on the essentials: the clear communication of content. It provides a wealth of examples and sample presentations, as well as a comprehensive manual (*The Beamer Class*, Tantau, Wright, and Miletic). However, in this chapter, we do not merely want to dedicate ourselves to the simple creation of presentations; we shall also strive to develop some expertise in the preparation, follow-up, and delivery of talks.

10.1 Preparing a Presentation

When you give a presentation, the audience only sees a fully developed set of slides and a (hopefully) inspiring speaker. However, most people are unaware of how much work is involved behind the scenes. A good presentation is not created while it is being delivered, but rather during the planning phase. Long before you stand in the spotlight, you can earn your success through systematic and thorough preparation. The preparation process can be divided into various phases, which we will examine in the following.

10.1.1 What is the Goal of the Presentation?

The first question you must ask and answer for yourself is the goal of the presentation. This involves a series of considerations that should be clarified at the outset:

- What do you actually want to communicate to your audience?
- Do you perhaps want to move the listeners to a specific action?
- Is a discussion round planned afterwards that should be stimulated by the introductory presentation?
- Or should information simply be conveyed?

All these questions must be answered in the first step, as the rest of the preparation is guided by them.

10.1.2 Who is the Audience?

This is also very important and should not be underestimated. On the one hand, the answer to this question determines the level at which the presentation should be held; on the other hand, it helps identify everything you might need to take into account. If you have an audience of specialists on the subject, you can assume a lot of detailed knowledge. If you have a group that has perhaps heard nothing about the topic so far, you must first summarise the basics and cannot reach the same depth. You should always consider the following points:

- What is the level of knowledge of the listeners?
- Is the audience international? (Language of the presentation)
- How high is the interest in the presentation?
- What does the audience expect from the presentation?
- What is the motivation of the listeners? (Are they attending the presentation voluntarily?)
- What is the audience's attitude towards the topic of the presentation?

A thorough analysis before the rest of the presentation planning brings many advantages. You can adapt the level of difficulty to the audience, as you are aware of their prior knowledge and their motivation to learn new things. The amount of content conveyed also depends heavily on this. A specialist audience with sufficient prior knowledge will still be able to follow a presentation at a higher level with more extensive content, whereas non-specialist listeners will quickly be left behind. This prevents you from talking past your audience.

If you can be sure in advance that the listeners will have a very critical attitude towards the topic of the presentation, you can also take precautions here. On the one hand, the prepared visualisations can be adapted accordingly; on the other hand, you can already gather arguments to defend your own point of view.

10.1.3 What is the Context of the Presentation?

Planning a presentation also involves taking the given context into account. The time frame is particularly important for the amount of information that can be conveyed. This includes not only the time available for the presentation itself. The timing is also significant, as the audience's concentration may be weakened after lunch or in the late afternoon. Furthermore, the size of the audience and the setup of the presentation room must be considered.

- How large is the presentation room?
- How many listeners are expected?
- How are the audience's seats arranged?
- Which media are available?
- Can or must a microphone be used?
- Is the presentation to be delivered from a lectern?

If your presentation is part of a larger series, you should also take the other speakers and their topics into account to ensure there are not too many overlaps.

If you are lucky enough to be able to define the context yourself, you can, of course, plan everything in the way that is most comfortable for you.

10.1.4 Collecting and Selecting Content

Once all other essential matters have been clarified, you can proceed to the content preparation. For an expert on the subject of the presentation, this is relatively straightforward. If you are preparing for a new topic, it will take longer and require more effort. In any case, the rule is to collect more information than will be used in the presentation so that you are also prepared for subsequent questions or a possible discussion. Sources such as books, journals, the internet, and certainly much more are available. (See, for example, Chapter 9.)

You should start by collecting a few key terms central to the presentation and then develop further material (information and graphical representations) and bullet points for these. In this way, all the information required for the presentation is gathered one by one.

10.1.5 Organising and Structuring Content

Once the research is complete, the content can now be appropriately sorted and summarised. In doing so, you should not include too much material. It is better to finish a presentation a few minutes early than to overrun your time.

You should build one or two buffer zones into your presentations, as disruptions to the process can easily occur. Organisational difficulties or failing technology can quickly lead to delays in the schedule. Furthermore, challenging questions from the audience or your own flow of speech – which can sometimes lead to spending too much time on a single point – can have a negative impact on the presentation time. In such cases, it is very practical if you can skip some details. However, you should never omit the core messages of the presentation.

Every presentation can be divided into three parts: introduction, main body, and conclusion. All three will be briefly described here.

Introduction: The introduction should motivate the audience. They should understand why they are attending this presentation and what benefits they will gain from it. They should be given an overview of what to expect during the talk.
The simplest approach is to first introduce yourself (unless this is done by a previous speaker or host) and then present the topic. At this stage, you can already provide a brief outlook on what exactly will be discussed. Following this, present the structure of the presentation with brief (!) explanations. The outline should

remain visible to the audience throughout the entire presentation. Now follows the introduction to the topic. This can be done using a current event or a historical entry point. In doing so, the importance of the topic should be particularly highlighted. For example, you can formulate open questions that you aim to answer in the course of the presentation.

Main Body: This is where the information the presentation is intended to contain is conveyed. This includes important background information and, especially, the objective you wish to work towards. All arguments and illustrations that explain the topic are introduced here. A "golden thread" is essential. You must work directly towards the objective without long digressions. Naturally, the level of difficulty must be adapted to the audience.

Conclusion: The end of the presentation should consist of a summary, conclusions, and an outlook. Care should be taken not to transition into this part too abruptly. It should already be heralded at the end of the main body, so that even those listeners who could not follow the "golden thread" until the end have the opportunity to at least understand the conclusion.
If a discussion is to follow the presentation, it is useful to summarise the important remaining open questions once more.
Following the presentation, questions often arise from the audience which should be clarified, or which may even trigger a longer discussion.

10.1.6 Planning and Creating Visualisations

A visualisation is intended to support a presentation with graphics and bullet points. Through the interplay of verbal (speech) and visual (presentation) information, many of the audience's senses are activated simultaneously. This increases receptivity enormously. The targeted use of images and graphics enhances clarity and, not least, persuasiveness. Visualisations are also a great help for the speaker themselves. During the presentation, they can serve as cue cards to help them stay on track.

However, such a method of presentation can also carry risks. The audience may devote too much of their attention to the presentation instead of following the talk itself. The blame for this is often found with the speakers themselves, as they become too preoccupied with the presentation and consequently lose essential (eye) contact with the audience. In particularly severe cases, the talk even appears as a perfect presentation with a rather secondary speaker. Alternatively, another extreme case occurs: the slides are overloaded with content and effects. These disadvantages must be avoided.

Keep the presentation simple: Much is already achieved if you design your presentation simply. Not everything that is possible must be applied. In this area especially, the rule is: less is more! Elaborate designs and effects distract the audience's attention from the content. When it comes to illustrations, it is better to use simplified schematic representations rather than fully realistic ones to ensure easy understanding. Furthermore, you should present exactly one train of thought per slide.

Use a consistent layout: Too much variety in the layout draws the audience's attention to itself. If a listener has to adapt to a new type of visualisation with every slide, they can no longer follow the essentials – namely, the content being conveyed.
In this regard, it is important to choose a plain, consistent background. A light background with dark lettering appears welcoming. Every slide should have the same spatial division. The heading must always be in the same position, and so on.
Only one font should be used throughout, and elements of the same type should always be set in the same font size. To specifically emphasise passages of text, the same type of marking should always be used.

Little text on slides: Each slide should have a heading that briefly and aptly summarises the statements made on that slide. The heading must stand out from the rest of the text, preferably through font size and emphasis.
Particular care must be taken to ensure that the text remains understandable. The use of bulleted lists is highly recommended. The following points must be strictly observed:

- Use bullet points, not full sentences
- Make unambiguous, precise statements
- A maximum of 10 lines per slide and a maximum of 10 words per line
- Sufficient line spacing and margins

Regarding the typeface, the use of normal script with upper- and lower-case letters is the obvious choice. Anything else is difficult to read and consequently causes the audience to become inattentive.

Colours: The use of colours is very important, as they make a visualisation varied and appeal to the audience's emotions. Everyone is familiar with the signaling effects of the colours green and red. We have already mentioned that light backgrounds appear particularly welcoming, whereas dark background colours tend to have a rather ominous effect on the audience. However, as we do not wish to delve into colour theory at this point, the reader is merely cautioned and referred to the numerous explanations found in other works.

Charts and Diagrams: Diagrams can support any statement. However, they must be clearly designed. It should be possible to recognise what is being depicted even without further explanation from the speaker. Axis labels and a legend are essential. Highly visible colours and line types must be used. Furthermore, overloading the image – which can sometimes occur even with as few as three graphs in a single diagram – should be avoided.

10.1.7 Developing a Manuscript

A distinction is made here between read-aloud and (semi-) extemporaneous presentations. Both versions, including their advantages and disadvantages, shall be briefly presented.

Read-aloud presentation:
In principle, it is possible to write a fully formulated script. Such a presentation has the advantage that it can be very precisely prepared and timed in advance. The risk of faltering or deviating from the topic during the presentation is very low. However, this method also makes one very inflexible. Spontaneous changes become virtually impossible. If you notice during the flow of speech that the presentation is failing to resonate with the audience, there is hardly any way to recover. A particularly serious disadvantage is the difficulty of writing a speech so that it also sounds good when spoken. Read-aloud presentations often sound stiff and lifeless. As a listener, one gets the impression that it would be better to read the text oneself. Therefore, it is preferable to avoid this form of presentation.

Extemporaneous or semi-extemporaneous presentation:

Another variant is a completely extemporaneous presentation. One has only the visualisations available and speaks freely without further aids.

A good middle ground is a semi-extemporaneous presentation supported by cue cards. When giving a presentation with slides, you can prepare a card for each slide, summarising the content to be conveyed in bullet points (no full sentences). These cards should not be too small and should be written on one side only, as they must be easy to read and should not cause confusion. Numbering and a descriptive heading are advantageous, as the stack of cards will almost certainly get mixed up more than once during preparation.

On the cards, you can highlight points that require special attention. Reminders of things the speaker must strictly observe can also appear on the card.

An ideal card size is A6, which can be used in landscape format. They should be made of slightly thicker paper, as they need to be very sturdy.

10.1.8 A Good Presentation Needs Practice

Even the most experienced speaker must go through their presentation in their mind several times. The correct sequence of the various points and the visualisations must be synchronised in the speaker's mind. The previously prepared cue cards should be used for assistance. Timing is also crucial. One should practice the presentation aloud several times beforehand, exactly as it would be delivered to an audience. This is the only way to be truly certain that the content and phrasing are sound and that the timing is correct. A rehearsal in front of a small, selected audience can also be beneficial. This provides many additional insights into potential misunderstandings and open questions.

10.1.9 Final Preparations Before the Presentation

Once the presentation has been written and practised, almost nothing stands in the way of a successful delivery. Only a few final preparations remain to be made.

One should endeavour to inspect and set up the presentation room some time before the talk begins. This allows you to prepare the room according to your requirements. It must be arranged so that both the speaker and the audience feel equally comfortable and the presentation can proceed without any hitches.

- You should explore and familiarise yourself with the room (e.g. the position of light switches, power sockets, etc.).
- The technical equipment to be used must be checked for functionality.
- Furniture and media can be moved and positioned according to your own preferences.
- The required materials must be laid out and ready.
- You can familiarise yourself with your position during the presentation in the empty room before the audience arrives.
- ...

All of this is intended to contribute to a smooth process and must be completed by the time the first listener arrives.

To slowly get used to being the centre of attention and to get to know your listeners better, it is advisable to be in the lecture room before the audience. In this way, the seats fill up only gradually, and it is easier to adjust to your role on the stage.

10.2 The LaTeX Beamer Package

The `beamer` package provides an environment for writing beamer presentations. Here, we aim to provide a brief introduction to its use. A complete description is provided by Tantau, Wright, and Miletic (beameruserguide.pdf). Additionally, the `xcolor` and `pgf` packages are required. Thus, the document header of a standard presentation becomes:

```
\documentclass{beamer}
\usepackage[latin1]{inputenc}
\usepackage[ngerman]{babel}
\usepackage{xcolor}
\usepackage{pgf}
...
```

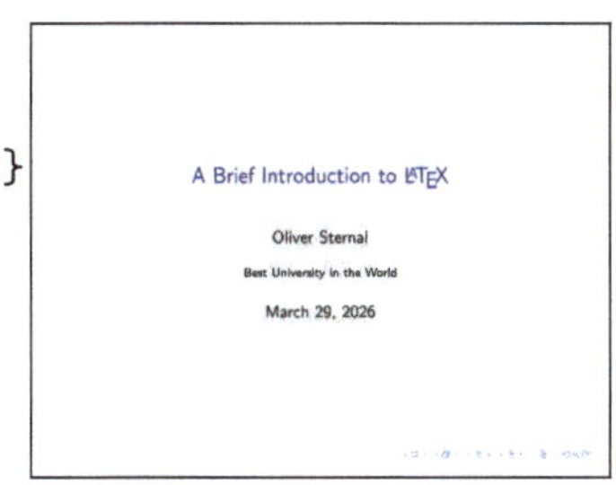

On the right-hand side, we also show the design of the title slide for the settings chosen in the header. The slide design can be changed very easily by incorporating various themes, some of which are supplied with the beamer package. To do this, simply insert the command \usetheme{theme} into the header, as shown here using the Warsaw theme as an example:

```
\documentclass{beamer}
\usetheme{Warsaw}
\usepackage[latin1]{inputenc}
\usepackage[ngerman]{babel}
\usepackage{xcolor}
\usepackage{pgf}
...
```

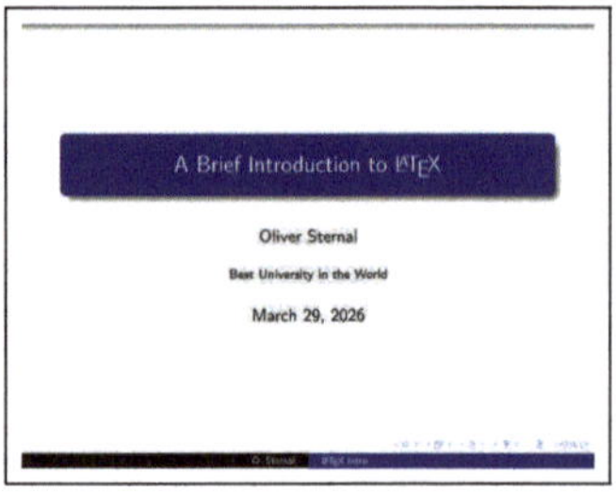

Many themes offer a wider selection of colour settings, which can be specified as an option in the document class. Let us use the red option of the Warsaw theme as an example:

```
\documentclass[red]{beamer}
\usetheme{Warsaw}
\usepackage[latin1]{inputenc}
\usepackage[ngerman]{babel}
\usepackage{xcolor}
\usepackage{pgf}
...
```

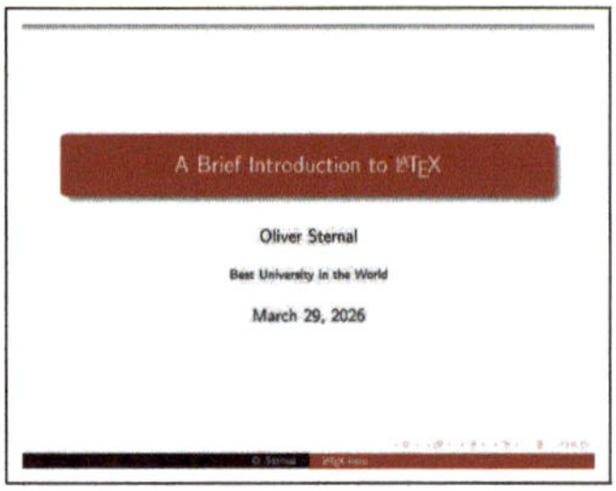

We will maintain these settings for the remaining examples.

10.2.1 The Title Material

In the document header, several important pieces of information about the presentation can be specified. Just as in any other document, the title, author, and date are set there. In this context, the possibility of using short versions for the title and author – which are specified in square brackets before the actual parameter – is extremely practical. Furthermore, the author's institutional affiliation can also be declared:

```
...
\title[\LaTeX\ Intro]{A Brief Introduction to \LaTeX}
\author[O. Sternal]{Oliver Sternal}
\institute{Best University in the World}
\date{March 29, 2026}
...
```

In anticipation of the next step in creating presentations, we want to generate the title frame (the title page) using the `\titlepage` command:

```
...
\title[\LaTeX\ Intro]{A Brief Introduction to \LaTeX}
\author[O. Sternal]{Oliver Sternal}
\institute{Best University in the World}
\date{March 29, 2026}
...
\begin{document}
\begin{frame}
  % title page
  \titlepage
\end{frame}
\end{document}
```

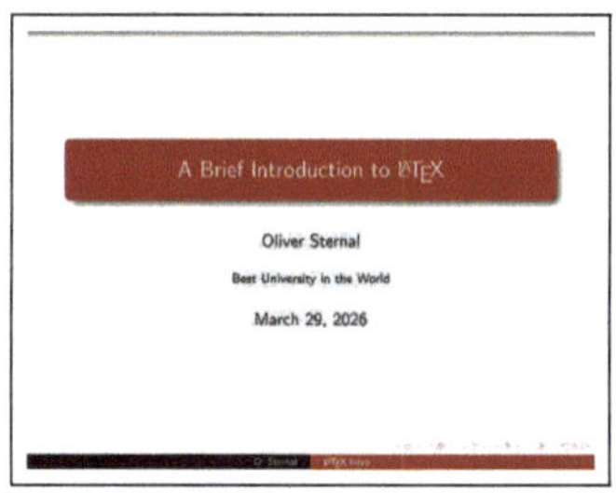

Die Kurzformen von Titel und Autor werden nun auf jeder Folie in der Fußzeile angezeigt.

10.2.2 The frame Environment

This brings us to the most important part: the creation of the slides that carry the content of the presentation. These are created using the `frame` environment:

```
\begin{frame}
\frametitle{Slide Title}
...
\end{frame}
```

Within this environment, the familiar rules for writing LaTeX documents apply.

```
\begin{frame}
\frametitle{Example Slide}
 The contents are presented
 on the following slides:
  \begin{itemize}
    \item Bullet points
    \item Images
    \item Grahs
    \item Tables
    \item \dots
  \end{itemize}
\end{frame}
```

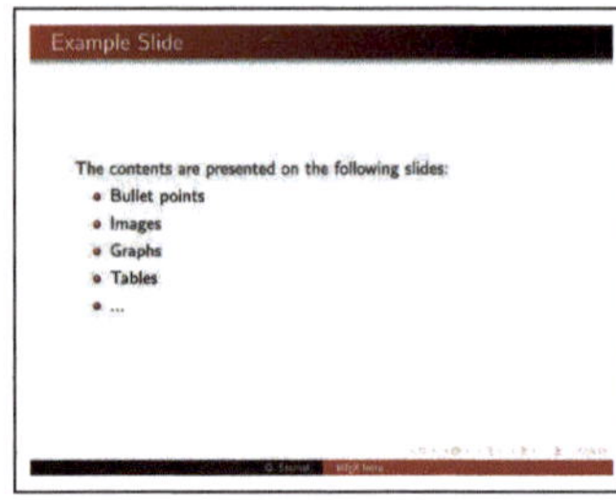

However, there are many more options available for designing the presentation, which we would like to address in the following sections.

10.2.3 Adding Structure to the Presentation

A presentation can – like any other document – be divided into `sections` and `subsections`. This division occurs *not* within the `frame` environments, but between them. A slide must be clearly assigned to a `section` or `subsection`. It is advisable to include a title slide for the new `section` following a `section` command, so that the audience is made aware of the beginning of the new section.

The table of contents is displayed in the header on every slide. From the audience's perspective, this is not unimportant, as it has a very positive effect when listeners always know which part of the presentation they are currently in and how much is still to come. (However, the `Warsaw` theme reserves a great deal of space for the table of contents on every slide, which can quickly become a disadvantage. You should therefore try out different themes and only then decide which one to use.)

A table of contents is generated as usual with the `\tableofcontents` command.

```
\begin{frame}
\frametitle{Table of Contents}
  \tableofcontents
\end{frame}
```

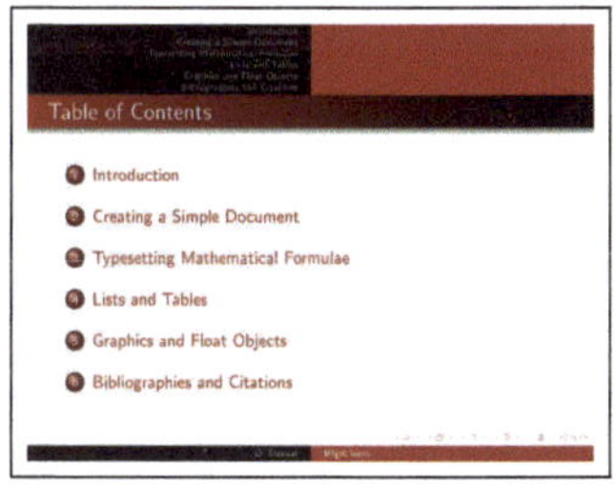

10.2.4 Creating Overlays

An important component of a presentation is overlays – the step-by-step build-up of the slide content. The simplest way to achieve this is with the \pause command. In this way, the build-up of the content is initially stopped at this command and only continued in the next step.

```
\begin{frame}
\frametitle{The \emph{pause} Command}
  The content of this slide is\\
  \pause
  built up using overlays.
\end{frame}
```

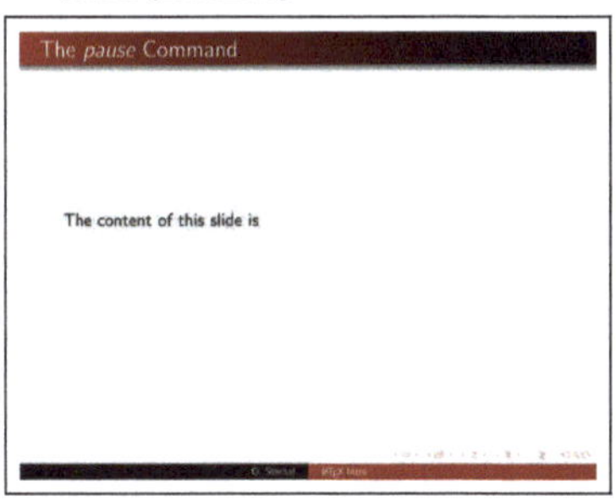

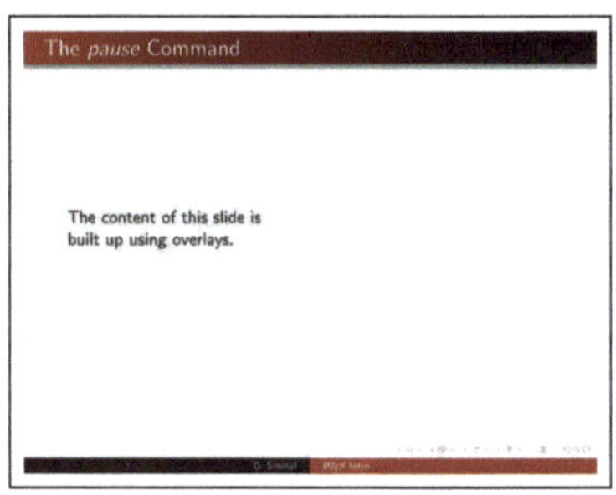

Another possibility is to use `\only<n-m>{content}`. In this case, n and m represent the first and last overlays of the slide on which the content within the curly brackets is displayed. If -m is omitted, the content is only shown on the n-th overlay. If only m is left out, the content appears from the n-th overlay until the end of the current frame. Using commas, it is also possible to create appearances across different overlays. The application is illustrated in the following example:

```
\begin{frame}
\frametitle{Slide Construction with
            the \emph{only} Command}
  \only<1,3>{Only in the 1st and 3rd slide\\}
  \only<2->{Displayed from the second slide onward\\}
  \only<2-3>{Visible on the 2nd and 3rd slide\\}
  \only<4>{Only on the fourth slide}
\end{frame}
```

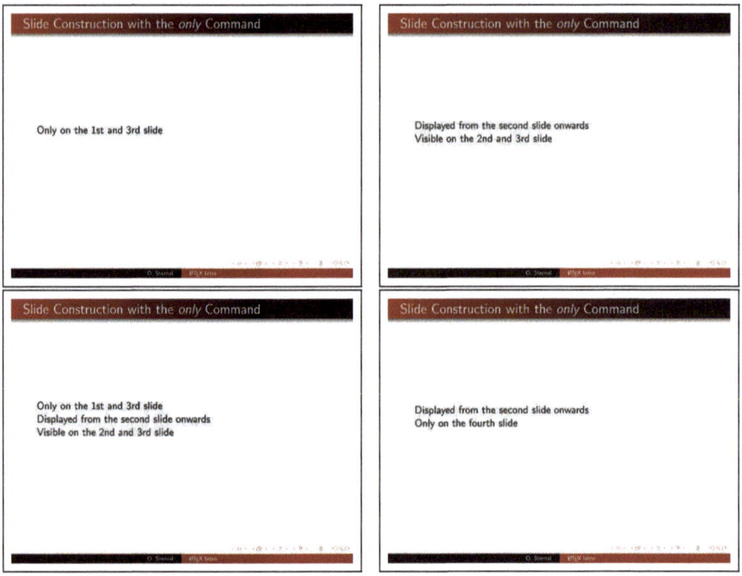

If you look very closely, you will notice that the `only` command reserves the space occupied by an element only for the specific slide for which the `only` command applies. This is particularly evident on the bottom two slides of the example.

Alternative commands to `\only` are listed here without examples. Their usage is identical to the `only` command. However, the difference lies in the fact that with the following commands, the required space on the slide is reserved from the very beginning. The names of the commands themselves should be self-explanatory.

```
\onslide<n-m>{Content appears on slides n to m.}
\uncover<n-m>{Content is uncovered from slide n to m.}
\visible<n-m>{Content is visible on slides n to m.}
\invisible<n-m>{Content is invisible from slide n to m.}
```

Some commands in beamer are provided with additional overlay options, such as bulleted and numbered lists:

```
\begin{frame}
\frametitle{Overlays in Lists}
  \begin{itemize}
  \item<1-> first point
  \item<1-> second point
  \item<2> third point
  \item<2> fourth point
  \end{itemize}
\end{frame}
```

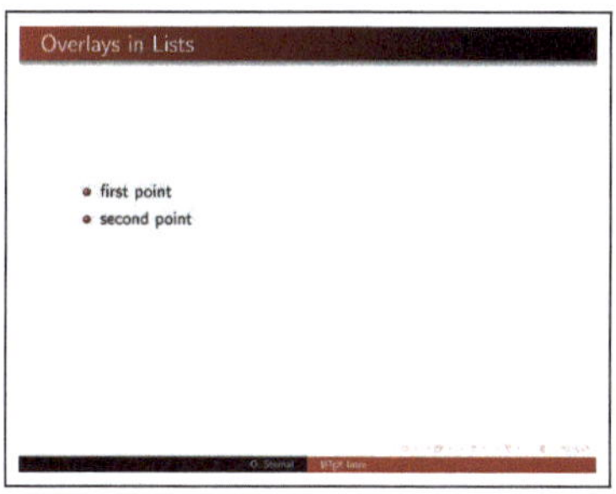

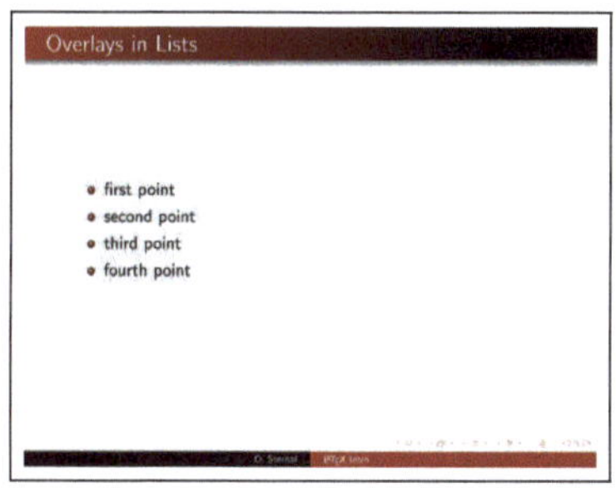

10.2.5 Organising Content on the Slide

By default, all content on the slides is vertically centred with the standard settings of the beamer package. This can be overridden by specifying an option in the document class. You can choose between vertical centring (c, default) and top alignment (t):

```
\documentclass[c]{beamer}
\documentclass[t]{beamer}
```

Using the columns environment, a slide can be divided into various columns. In this case, the width must be specified in curly brackets for each individual column. If the width is omitted, LaTeX will issue an error.

```
\begin{frame}
\frametitle{Slide with Column Layout}
  \begin{columns}[T]
    \begin{column}{0.3\textwidth}
      Left column
    \end{column}
    \begin{column}{0.4\textwidth}
      Middle column
    \end{column}
    \begin{column}{0.3\textwidth}
      Right column
    \end{column}
  \end{columns}
\end{frame}
```

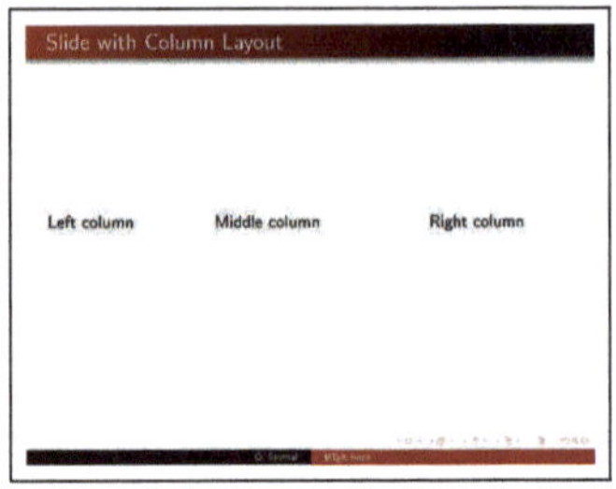

10.2.6 Animations and Videos

Animations can be inserted and played from external sources or created by displaying a sequence of different overlays on a single slide. The latter is achieved using the `\animate<n-m>` command, where `n` and `m` represent the first and last overlays belonging to the animation, respectively. If `n = 1`, the first overlay of the slide is included in the animation, and the animation starts as soon as the corresponding slide is accessed. Tip: Just try it out and play around with it a little.

```
\begin{frame}
\frametitle{Animation}
\animate<2-m>
\only<1>{\includegraphics{image_1.jpg}}
\only<2>{\includegraphics{image_2.jpg}}
\only<3>{\includegraphics{image_3.jpg}}
...
\only<m>{\includegraphics{image_m.jpg}}
\only<m+1>{\includegraphics{image_m+1.jpg}}
\end{frame}
```

In the animation presented here, the sequence is animated from the second to the penultimate overlay. This means that the first image is initially displayed as a static slide. At the next slide transition, the animation runs from the second to the m-th image, after which the last image is shown statically again. (Caution: Not every PDF viewer displays these animations as intended. If you plan to use such animations for your presentation, you should definitely test them in your PDF viewer.)

Videos can also be integrated into a presentation. The `media9` and `multimedia` packages provide excellent assistance. You can find the manuals for these very easily online.

10.2.7 Further Commands and Environments

Up to this point, we have been able to provide a brief insight into designing presentations with LaTeX Beamer. Naturally, this package offers many more possibilities. The internet provides numerous extensions. However, even a quick glance at the package manual (Tantau, Wright, and Miletić, beameruserguide.pdf) reveals far more than can be explained here.

10.3 A Brief Introduction to Presentation Techniques

This topic is not intended to deal with the actual content of a presentation, but rather with the speaker and their conduct before an audience. But before we dive straight in, let us ask ourselves what we expect from a speaker. In addition to technical competence, this includes a confident manner and a polite interaction with the audience. A presenter should be honest and enjoy what they are doing. Only then will they be able to convince us of the points addressed in the presentation.

From our own perceptions of what makes a good presentation, we can certainly deduce the desired conduct of a speaker. So, what qualities should a good presenter possess?

10.3.1 Clarity and Intelligibility

One should speak freely and clearly. Technical terms and abbreviations should always be explained. The essential points of the presentation must be highlighted distinctly. High levels of clarity are achieved through the use of figurative language and good examples.

Pauses are an important rhetorical device. By taking a short break as a speaker, you give the audience a chance to reflect briefly on the content conveyed so far and to understand it better. This short period also allows questions to arise, the clarification of which may be important for the further course of the presentation. Everyone else, as well as the speaker themselves, can take a breath and recover briefly during this time.

10.3.2 Encouraging the Audience

The audience will be best able to follow a presentation if they are encouraged to think along. To achieve this, one can involve the listeners in a short discussion or ask targeted questions. If a speaker conducts themselves with great energy and shows initiative and commitment, they will command a great deal of attention from their audience. This includes, in particular, a witty demeanour. It is better to work with surprising and novel examples than to use clichés that everyone now finds tedious. Humorous references should be as much a part of the presentation as simple yet profound questions.

10.3.3 Creating a Good Atmosphere

The audience expects a cooperative approach from their speaker. All listeners must be taken seriously; there are no such things as "stupid questions". Even when finding oneself in an unaccustomed, prominent role, one must not be rattled by anything. With a positive underlying attitude, navigating a presentation becomes significantly easier. It earns a great deal of goodwill if one is able to share a laugh with the audience.

10.3.4 Body Language

This is among the most important aspects a speaker must consider. There are many dos and don'ts, some of which depend heavily on the cultural context. In America, for example, it was long considered incredibly casual for a speaker to keep one hand in their pocket. (Perhaps that is still the case today?) However, in large parts of the rest of the world, this gesture is regarded as disrespectful. (In Germany, there is even a colloquial saying: "The speaker is playing pocket billiards.")

All in all, it can only be said that as a speaker, you must feel comfortable. You should not do anything that you do not want to do yourself. However, you should also avoid gestures that appear disrespectful to the audience. Nevertheless, some behaviours are of fundamental importance:

- Eye contact with the entire (!) audience ensures attention. One should not constantly look back and forth or remain fixed on one's own presentation, but rather let one's gaze sweep slowly over the audience and linger on a few faces for a while.

- A firm, upright stance demonstrates a steady point of view to the audience, as well as the necessary thematic confidence and conviction. Many speakers sway a great deal or frequently take a few steps forwards and backwards or to the side. This habit should be broken as quickly as possible.

- Gestures and facial expressions must match the presentation. One should ensure that gestures take place in the "positive zone", i.e., at the level of the upper body. Gestures performed too low appear negative, while at head height, they can seem excessively positive or preachy. Gestures and facial expressions are very important, as they show that a speaker is physically engaged with their presentation. They assist the speaker in convincing the audience.

- The voice must be adapted to the room. One must speak loudly, clearly, and dynamically. Nothing is as soporific as a presentation delivered monotonically without any emphasis.

- In very large lecture halls, a microphone must be used, creating one of those rare situations in which one hears one's own voice. Therefore, it is sensible to practise using a microphone beforehand and to get used to the sound of one's own voice, which many people find very difficult. But as a comfort to them: our fellow human beings always hear us that way!

There are many rules of conduct when facing an audience, but the most important rule is surely this: always be yourself. Someone who suddenly behaves differently in front of an audience appears untrustworthy.

10.3.5 Dealing with Mishaps

Every speaker encounters various mistakes during a presentation. Usually, the flow of thought or words gets jumbled, or a technical glitch occurs. In any of these cases, only a little time – usually just a few seconds – is needed to reorganise one's thoughts, find the right phrasing, or fix a brief technical failure. The key is to remain calm and gain the necessary time. This can be achieved in several ways. One can...

- ...repeat the last train of thought.

- ...give a brief summary of the most important points so far.

- ... ask the audience a question.

Especially during a brief blackout, it is very helpful to repeat the last few thoughts. In most cases, this provides enough time to recover the next point and proceed with the presentation.

If a mishap occurs, the most important thing is not to leave yourself at the mercy of the audience. Only very few listeners will notice an error, as they are unfamiliar with the planned sequence of the presentation. After all, this is known only to the presenter. Therefore, a speaker can simply skip over forgotten, less important points without the audience noticing. It would be far worse to alert the audience to a mistake by saying, "I just forgot to tell you something there..." or "Oh, I seem to have lost my train of thought..."

A speaker must always be emotionally prepared for mistakes, as they happen more than once even to the most experienced presenters. It is of little help to focus solely on avoiding mishaps, as this quickly makes the presentation appear strained. The best approach is simply to stay relaxed. Particularly in the field of talks and presentations, the following principle applies: maximum coolness in the face of maximum uncertainty.

10.3.6 Questions at the Conclusion

If you have delivered an interesting presentation, you must expect questions from the audience. These are a great compliment to the speaker, as they show that they have succeeded in piquing the listeners' interest. Initially, one often needs a little time to search for the right answer. This can be achieved by repeating the question for the rest of the audience or by acknowledging it (e.g., "You raise a very interesting point there..."). Especially for the sake of those listeners who may not have a keen interest in the specific question asked, an answer should be brief and precise. When answering, one should not focus solely on the questioner, as this can easily lead to losing contact with the rest of the audience.

If answering a question goes too far or could lead to an extensive discussion, you should politely point out to the questioner that a full answer would require a lengthy explanation and offer to be available for further information after the presentation. Nevertheless, a short version of the answer should still be provided.

If you do not have an answer to a question to hand, you should not try to talk around the question or evade it. Such an attempt is usually noticed immediately, and the speaker quickly appears incompetent. Instead, one should directly admit one's lack of knowledge, indicate one's own interest in an explanation, and offer to find an answer "to this interesting question".

If a question is asked during the presentation that will be clarified later on, you should ask the questioner to be patient for a little while longer. Once you finally reach the relevant point in the talk, you should refer back to the question, as the audience can often remember that a question was asked, but not necessarily its content. Without an additional reference, the question will remain in the audience's mind as unanswered, which tends to lead to a negative assessment of the speaker.

After a question during the presentation, it is essential to briefly repeat the current train of thought. This ensures that all listeners are back on the same page and can continue to follow the talk.

10.4 Follow-up to the Presentation

When the presentation is long over for the audience, the final part begins for the speaker. One should take sufficient time for a reflection on the entire event. In doing so, several questions should be answered:

- Was the goal achieved?
- Were the interests of the audience met?
- Was the process (from the start of the planning phase to the end of the talk) successful?
- How successful were the individual parts of the presentation?
- Could all listeners follow the explanations in the main body?
- Was it possible to engage all listeners equally?
- Were there any critical situations of a technical or subject-related nature?
- What were the reactions of the audience after the presentation?
- Were the organisation, room, and time planning successful?

A direct and thorough follow-up to the presentation is essential and provides the opportunity to learn for future talks. With this phase, the presentation is finally concluded for the speaker as well.

Chapter 11

Designing Graphics with PGF and TikZ

In academic work, the clear and precise presentation of data, theoretical models, and complex relationships is indispensable. The *PGF* (Portable Graphics Format) system, and its frontend *TikZ* in particular, offers a flexible way to create high-quality vector graphics directly within LaTeX. In contrast to embedding externally created images, this guarantees a *consistent font* and seamless integration into the document layout.

11.1 Fundamentals of TikZ

`TikZ` is a LaTeX package for creating graphics directly within the LaTeX source code. During compilation, LaTeX then generates a vector graphic that is embedded directly into the document. To this end, the package provides a simple command syntax for drawing lines, shapes, arrows, and text nodes.

To create graphics with `TikZ`, the corresponding package must be included:

```
\usepackage{tikz}
```

A drawing is then designed using the appropriate commands within the `tikzpicture` environment. The design is based on Cartesian coordinates, where the coordinates (x, y) are specified in parentheses. The coordinate system itself is not displayed in the images. One centimetre

(1 cm) is used as the default unit of length. Let's look at this in a simple example where we draw a straight line:

```
\begin{tikzpicture}
  % Draw a line from
  % (0,0) to (3,2)
  \draw (0,0) -- (3,2);
\end{tikzpicture}
```

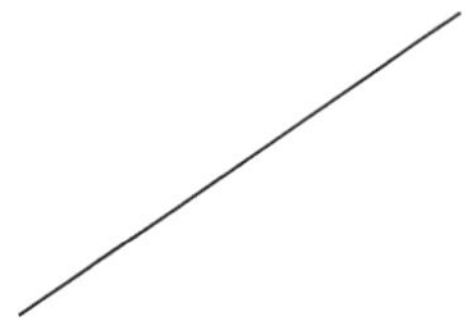

In this example, we already see the use of the \draw command, followed by a chain of path operations that must end with a semicolon. Rectangles or circles can be drawn in a similar fashion.

```
\begin{tikzpicture}
% Draw a rectangle with the
% corners (0,0) and (2,1)
\draw (0,0) rectangle (2,1);
\end{tikzpicture}
```

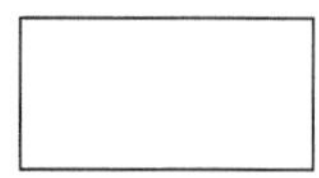

```
\begin{tikzpicture}
% Draw a circle with
% centre (0,0) and radius 2
\draw (0,0) circle (2);

% Draw another circle with
% centre (1,0) and radius 1
\draw (1,0) circle (1);
\end{tikzpicture}
```

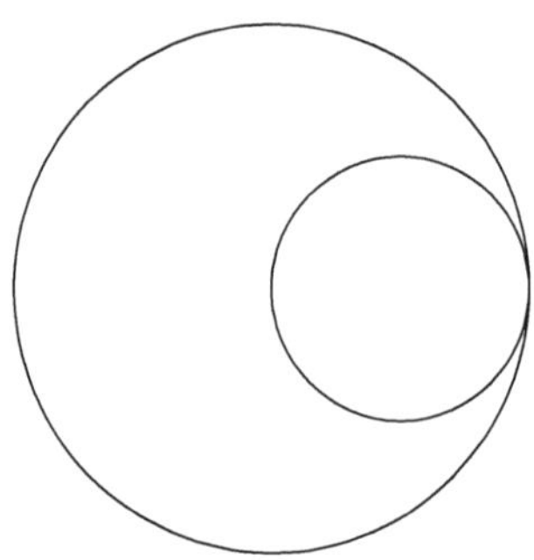

Additional options such as colour, line width, or filling are appended to the \draw command in square brackets:

```
\begin{tikzpicture}
  % Draw a red circle with
  % centre (0,0) and radius 2
  \draw[red,very thick] (0,0) circle (2);

  % Draw a blue circle with
  % centre (1,0) and radius 1
  \draw[blue, line width=0.8mm] (1,0) circle (1);
\end{tikzpicture}
```

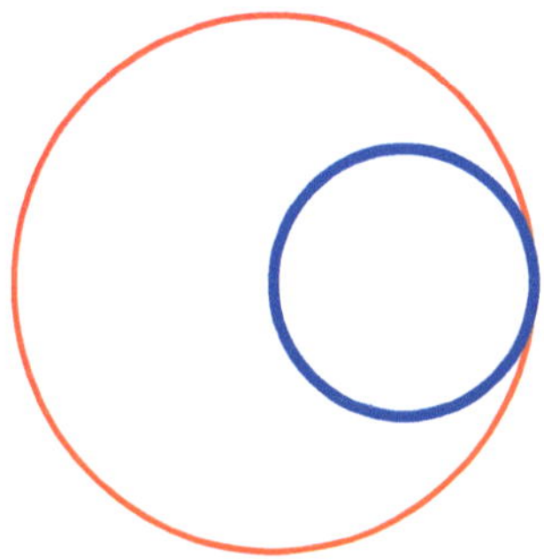

In the last example, two different ways of setting the line thickness were used. `TikZ` offers a choice between predefined line widths and a manual setting using the `line width=X` option. In this case, a value for the line thickness including a unit, e.g., `line width=0.3cm` or `line width=2pt`, is inserted for `X`. The predefined line widths are shown in Table 11.1. The default value is the line thickness `thin`.

`ultra thin`:	0.1pt	`very thin`:	0.2pt
`thin`:	0.4pt	`semithick`:	0.6pt
`thick`:	0.8pt	`very thick`:	1.2pt
`ultra thick`:	1.6pt		

Table 11.1: Predefined line widths and their assigned values

Using the `fill=X` option, geometric shapes can also be filled with colours or patterns. In this case, `X` is replaced by a colour option. For example, one of the predefined colours

`red`, `green`, `blue`, `cyan`, `magenta`, `yellow`, `black`, `white`, `gray`, `orange`, `brown`, `pink`, `violet`, `olive`, `teal` oder `lime` can be used. However, it is also possible to mix colours. Light and dark shades are created by mixing with white or black, respectively; however, mixtures of any colours are also possible.

```
\begin{tikzpicture}
  % Draw different circles with
  % various fill colours
  %
  \draw[fill=red, very thick] (0,2) circle (1);
  %
  \draw[fill=red!40, very thick] (2,2) circle (1);
  %
  \draw[fill=red!70!black, very thick] (4,2) circle (1);
  %
  \draw[fill=red!25!blue, very thick] (0,0) circle (1);
  %
  \draw[fill=red!75!blue, very thick] (2,0) circle (1);
  %
  \draw[fill=black!40, very thick] (4,0) circle (1);
\end{tikzpicture}
```

Various shades of grey are produced by mixing black and white. The line colour can also be influenced in the same way. Table 11.2 explains the colour mixing:

The TikZ package can be loaded with various libraries. For filling geometric shapes, for example, the patterns library is popular. With the shadings library, colour gradients can be created:

```
\usetikzlibrary{patterns, shadings}
```

The following example shows the use of some patterns and gradients:

`red`	Use of the base colour red.
`red!40`	Mixes red with white and creates a light red. Proportions: 40% red, 60% white.
`red!70!black`	Mixes red with black and creates a dark red. Proportions: 70% red, 30% black.
`red!25!blue`	Mixes red with blue and creates a violet shade. Proportions: 25% red, 75% blue.
`red!75!blue`	Mixes red with blue and creates a violet shade. Proportions: 75% red, 25% blue.
`black!40`	Mixes black with white and creates a shade of grey. Proportions: 40% black, 60% white.

Table 11.2: Explanation of colour mixing

```
\begin{tikzpicture}
  % Draw various circles with
  % different patterns
  %
  \draw[pattern=dots, very thick] (0,2) circle (1);
  %
  \draw[pattern=checkerboard, pattern color=blue] (2,2)
    circle (1);
  %
  \draw[pattern=north east lines, very thick] (4,2)
    circle (1);
  %
  \draw[pattern=north west lines, very thick] (0,0)
    circle (1);
  %
  \draw[top color=red, bottom color=blue] (2,0)
   circle (1);
  %
  \draw[inner color=white, outer color=black] (4,0)
    circle (1);
  %
\end{tikzpicture}
```

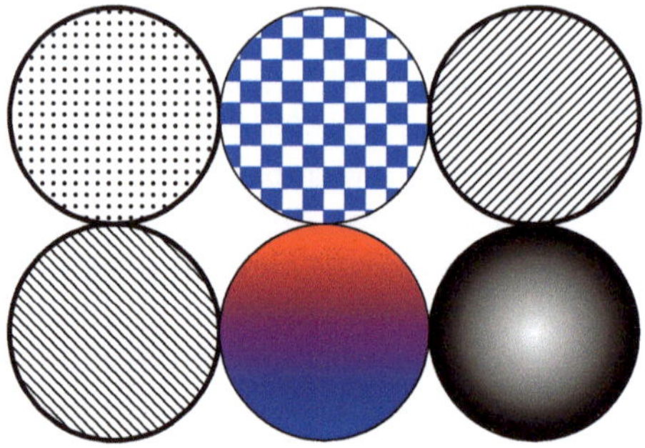

11.2 Further Geometric Shapes

In addition to straight lines, rectangles, and circles, TikZ also offers commands for more complex shapes:

Path operations	Generated shape
(x, y) ellipse (rx and ry)	Creates an ellipse with the radii rx and ry.
(x1, y1) arc (a1:a2:r)	Creates a circular arc with radius r from angle a1 to angle a2 measured relative to the horizontal.
(x1,y1) parabola (x2,y2)	Creates a parabola between points (x1,y1) and (x2,y2) with the vertex at the starting point.
(x1,y1) .. controls (c1,c2) and (d1,d2) .. (x2,y2)	Creates a Bézier curve with starting point (x1,y1) and end point (x2,y2). The curve leaves the starting point towards control point (c1,c2) and reaches the end point from the direction of control point (d1,d2).

These shapes are shown in the following examples:

```
\begin{tikzpicture}
  %
  \draw (0,0) ellipse (1.5 and 0.5);
  %
\end{tikzpicture}
```

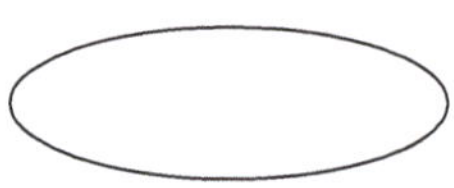

```
\begin{tikzpicture}
  %
  \draw (0,0) arc (20:240:1);
  %
\end{tikzpicture}
```

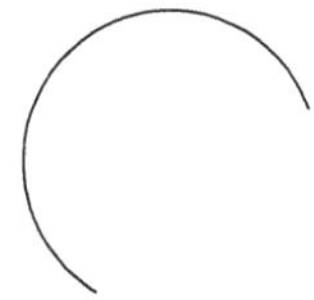

```
\begin{tikzpicture}
  %
  \draw (0,-1) parabola (3,1);
  %
\end{tikzpicture}
```

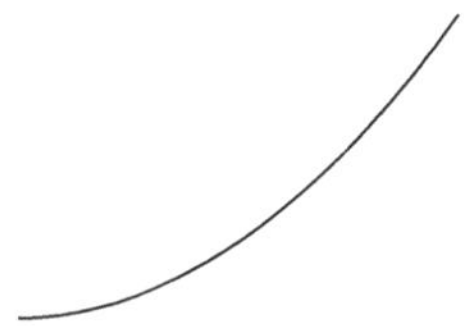

```
\begin{tikzpicture}
  %
  \draw (0,-1) .. controls (2,1) and (4,-4) .. (6,0.5);
  %
\end{tikzpicture}
```

11.3 Advanced Elements

An important element of TikZ drawings are nodes. Nodes are used to position text, symbols, or graphics at specific coordinates within an image, allowing these elements to be easily connected to each other later on. To achieve this, a node is defined at a coordinate point within the tikzpicture using the \node command:

```
\node[options] (name) at (x,y) {content}
```

This command defines a node at the coordinates (x,y) and assigns a name by which this node can be referenced. Content in the form of text, symbols, or graphics can be inserted at the node. Empty content is also permitted. The use of nodes is shown in the following example:

```
\begin{tikzpicture}
  % Node at (0, 0) with a border around the text
  \node[draw, rounded corners, fill=green!30]
        at (0, 0) (A) {Centre};

  % Node at (-4, 0)
  \node[circle, draw, fill=violet!50] at (-4, 0) (B) {Left};

  % Node at (0, 4)
  \node[circle, draw, fill=red!30] at (0, 4) (C) {Top};

  % Node at (4, 0)
  \node[circle, draw, fill=teal!40] at (4, 0) (D) {Right};

  % Connection between the nodes (arrow)
  \draw[->, very thick] (A) -- (C);
  \draw[<-, very thick] (A) -- (B);
  \draw[<->, very thick] (A) -- (D);
  \draw[->, very thick, rounded corners] (B) -- (-4,4) -- (C);
  \draw[<->, very thick] (D) -- (C);
\end{tikzpicture}
```

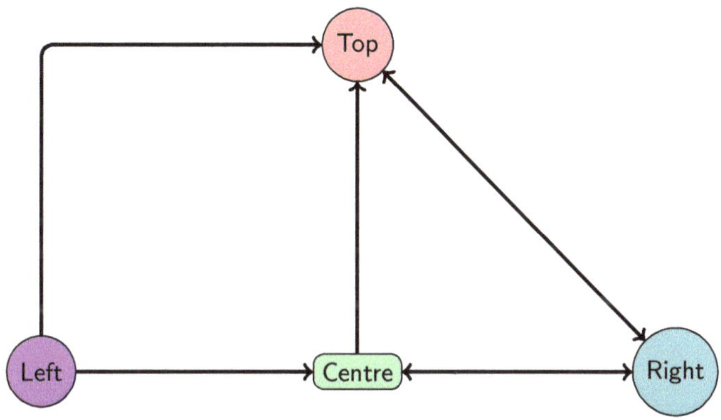

The following example shows the use of loops using the labelling of coordinate axes as an example. The loop begins with the `\foreach` command and the assignment of the counter variable `\i` and its values:

```
\foreach \i in {list of assigned values}
```

The variable name can be chosen freely. The subsequent command is executed for the values in the list, where the variable can be used in coordinates and in texts.

Furthermore, the `scale` option for the `tikzpicture` environment is introduced here. This allows for the scaling of the generated image by a fixed factor.

```
\begin{tikzpicture}[scale=1.2]
  % 1. Draw a coordinate system
  \draw[->] (-4, 0) -- (4, 0) node[below] {x};
  \draw[->] (0, -2) -- (0, 2) node[left] {f(x)};

  % 2. Use a loop to label the x-axis
  \foreach \i in {-3, -2, -1, 1, 2, 3}
    \draw (\i, -0.1) -- (\i, 0.1);
  \foreach \i in {-3, -2, -1, 1, 2, 3}
    \draw (\i, -0.3) node {\i};

  % 3. Use a loop to label the y-axis
  \foreach \i in {-1, 1}
    \draw (0.1, \i) -- (-0.1, \i);
  \foreach \i in {-1, 1}
    \draw (-0.3, \i) node {\i};
\end{tikzpicture}
```

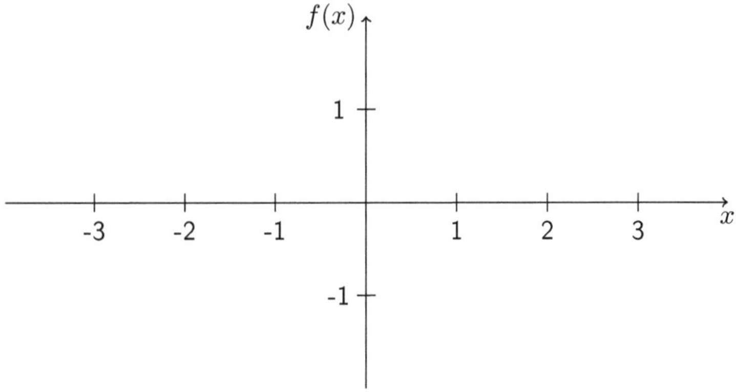

We use the example shown above to represent a graph and some data points. To implement these examples, the calc library is required:

```
\usetikzlibrary{calc}
```

To draw a function graph, we use the \draw plot command with several options:

```
\draw[blue,thick,domain=-3.5:3.5,samples=200]
     plot (\x,{sin(\x*180/pi)});
```

The domain = x1:x2 option defines the domain over which the function graph is drawn. The graph starts at x= x1 and ends at x= x2. The samples option specifies the number of sample points at which the values of the function to be drawn are calculated.

The command

```
\fill[red] (\i, 0.25*\i) circle (1.5pt);
```

draws red-filled circles at the coordinates (\i, 0.25*\i).

```
\begin{tikzpicture}[scale=1.2]
  % 1. Draw a coordinate system
  \draw[->] (-4, 0) -- (4, 0) node[below] {$x$};
  \draw[->] (0, -2) -- (0, 2) node[left] {$f(x)$};

  % 2. Use a loop to label the x-axis
  \foreach \i in {-3, -2, -1, 1, 2, 3}
      \draw (\i, -0.1) -- (\i, 0.1);
  \foreach \i in {-3, -2, -1, 1, 2, 3}
      \draw (\i, -0.3) node {\i};

  % 3. Use a loop to label the y-axis
  \foreach \i in {-1, 1}
      \draw (0.1, \i) -- (-0.1, \i);
  \foreach \i in {-1, 1}
      \draw (-0.3, \i) node {\i};

  % 4. Draw the function f(x) = sin(x)
  \draw[blue,thick,domain=-3.5:3.5,samples=200]
       plot (\x,{sin(\x*180/pi)});

  % 5. Draw data points at (i, 0.25*i)
  \foreach \i in {-3, -2, -1, 0, 1, 2, 3}
      \fill[red] (\i, 0.25*\i) circle (1.5pt);
\end{tikzpicture}
```

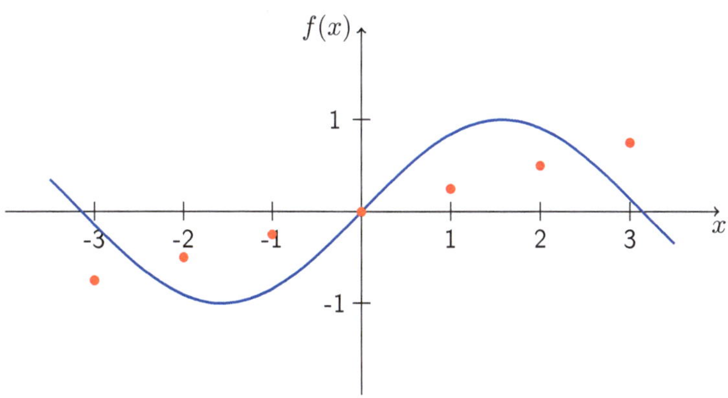

11.4 Diagrams and Plots with pgfplots

The TikZ package is very well suited for schematic diagrams and sketches. For the representation of function graphs and data, the pgfplots package is also frequently used. This package was specifically developed for creating graphs based on mathematical data and functions.

The pgfplots package must be loaded in addition to TikZ. However, with this package, it is important to additionally specify a version number using \pgfplotsset{compat=X} to guarantee that LaTeX uses modern standards during conversion. Please stay informed about the current development status of the package when using pgfplots.

Many modern online tools and mathematics programmes allow graphs to be exported as source code for TikZ and pgfplots. This makes the application even more convenient.

```
\usepackage{pgfplots}
\pgfplotsset{compat=1.18}
```

Graphs are placed within an axis environment, which in turn must be located within a tikzpicture environment. A simple function graph can be created using the \addplot command by specifying the function directly. pgfplots automatically handles the axis labelling and scaling.

```
\begin{tikzpicture}
\begin{axis}[xlabel=$x$, ylabel=$f(x)$, grid=both,
             minor tick num = 3]
    % Graph of the function f(x) = x^2 - 1 in the
    % range from -2 to 2
    \addplot[blue, thick, domain=-2:2] {x^2 - 1};
\end{axis}
\end{tikzpicture}
```

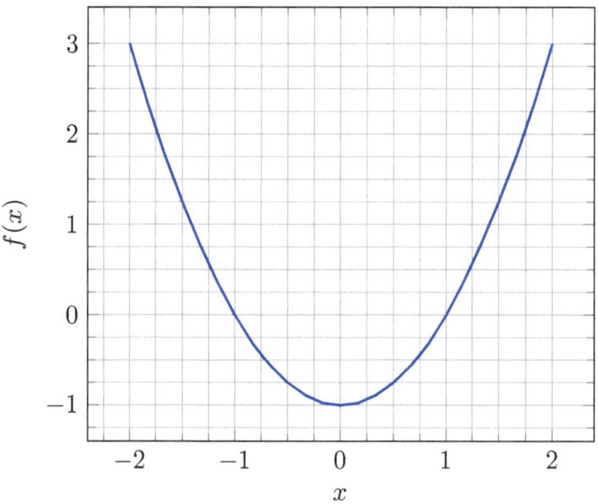

Here, the grid option determines the design of the grid:

grid = none:	No grid is drawn. (Default)
grid = major:	Draws lines at the positions of the major tick labels.
grid = minor:	Draws lines at the smaller intermediate marks (minor ticks).
grid = both:	Draws both sets of grid lines.

The minor tick num option specifies the number of minor tick marks between the major tick labels.

A function graph can, of course, also be drawn in a coordinate system with coordinate axes instead of a grid:

```
\begin{tikzpicture}
\begin{axis}[axis lines=middle, xlabel=$x$,
             ylabel=$f(x)$, domain=-2:2, samples=200]
    % Graph of the function f(x) = x^2 - 1 in the
    % range from -2 to 2
    \addplot[blue, thick] {x^2 - 1};
\end{axis}
\end{tikzpicture}
```

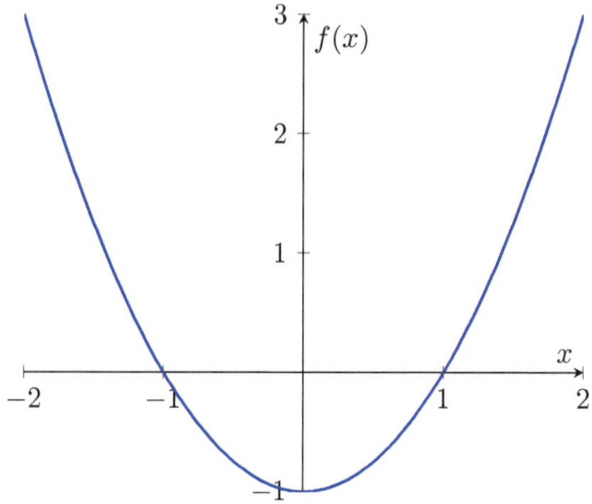

Data can also be specified directly in the LaTeX file and plotted. This is ideal for ensuring consistency between measured values and their representation. The following example is provided, which also introduces the use of a legend:

```
\begin{tikzpicture}
\begin{axis}[
    title=Temperature Measurement,
    xlabel=time (s),
    ylabel=temperature (K),
    legend pos=south east,
    ymajorgrids=true,
]
    % Data points as red circles
    \addplot[black, mark=o, mark size=2pt, only marks]
             coordinates {
               (1, 273.15)
               (2, 275.50)
               (3, 279.90)
               (4, 281.25)
             };
    \addlegendentry{Experiment A}
\end{axis}
\end{tikzpicture}
```

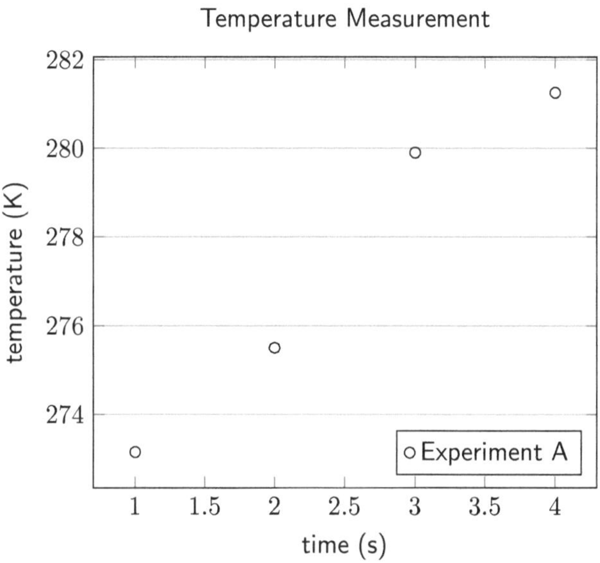

The `only marks` option ensures that the data points are not connected. If this option is omitted, the data points are connected with straight lines. The symbols of the data points can be adjusted using the `mark` option:

`mark=`	filled circle
`mark=o`	open circle
`mark=square`	open square
`mark=square`	filled square
`mark=triangle`	open triangle
`mark=triangle*`	filled triangle
`mark=diamond`	open diamond
`mark=diamond*`	filled diamond
`mark=x`	cross
`mark=+`	plus sign

The limit for the number of data points depends on the compiler (pdfLaTeX, LuaLaTeX, XeLaTeX) used to convert the source text.

Chapter 12

PDF Documents with Interactive Elements

Some interactive elements can certainly be helpful in scientific documents. These include, in particular, internal links for cross-references, links to websites outside the document, or bookmarks. Furthermore, there are several other interactive elements (e.g. form fields or buttons) that can be useful but are not necessarily required in a scientific document. Some of these possibilities will be discussed in this chapter.

12.1 Fundamentals: The hyperref Package

The `hyperref` package forms the foundation for creating interactive PDF documents. It serves as the basis for hyperlinks, bookmarks, form fields, and buttons. The package should be included at the end of the

`linkcolor`:	Colour of internal links (cross-references to chapters, figures, tables, etc.)
`citecolor`:	Colour of citations in the text (links to the bibliography)
`urlcolor`:	Colour of web addresses (links to websites or email links)

Table 12.1: Colour options for various link types in the PDF document

preamble:

```
\usepackage[hidelinks]{hyperref}
```

The hidelinks option is often chosen to suppress the boxes that are otherwise displayed around links. These are perceived as distracting, particularly in printed documents. However, the hidelinks option hides links completely, so they can no longer be distinguished from normal text – provided, of course, that no colours have been assigned to the various link types.

```
\usepackage[colorlinks=true,urlcolor=blue]{hyperref}
```

In PDF documents, a distinction is made between various link types, each of which can be styled with its own colour option (see Table 12.1).

The inclusion of the hyperref package has several automatic effects:

Navigation: All entries in the table of contents, list of figures, and list of tables are provided with links. Readers can navigate within the PDF document by clicking on the entries in these lists.

Cross-references: All cross-references created with \ref can be used to navigate to the corresponding point in the document linked with \label by clicking on them.

PDF Bookmarks: A navigation structure for PDF readers is created, which allows for the setting of bookmarks.

Furthermore, the hyperref package can also be used to include URLs and email links:

```
% URL-Link:
\url{https://www.example.com}

% Email-Link:
\href{mailto:someone@example.com}{Email to the author}
```

https://www.example.com
Email to the author

12.2 Form Elements with the hyperref Package

This section introduces the form functions of the hyperref package, which can be used to create forms with fillable fields.

`name`:	Unique ID. Required for data processing when saving the completed form.
`width`:	Width of the input area
`height`:	Height of the input area
`bordercolor`:	Colour of the border
`multiline=true`:	Allows multi-line text in the form field.
`value`:	Defines the default text pre-filled in the form field.

Table 12.2: Attributes of the text field

Text Fields

A text field for entering free text is created using the `\TextField` command:

```
Name: \TextField[width=5cm, bordercolor=black,
                 name=Name1]{}
```

Name:

Table 12.2 shows the various attributes that can be given to a text field to adapt it to one's own needs. It is important to note here that adjusting the height of the input field is not sufficient to enable multi-line input. If the input field is to allow multi-line text, the option `multiline=true` must be used.

```
\begin{tabular}{p{2cm}p{6cm}}
Free text: & \raisebox{-0.8cm}
                 {\TextField[width=5cm, height=1cm,
                             multiline=true,
                             bordercolor=black,
                             name=freetext]{}}
\end{tabular}
```

Free text:

Since the bottom line of the input field is aligned with the baseline of the letters in the text, this part of the form was arranged using a table and a `raisebox`.

Checkboxes

Checkboxes allow for the selection of binary options (yes/no) by placing tick marks in the boxes. If several boxes are used in a form, they can be selected independently of one another:

```
\CheckBox[name=OptionTAC, checked]
   {I have read the terms and conditions: }\\
\CheckBox[name=OptionNews]
   {I would like to subscribe to the newsletter: }
```

I have read the terms and conditions: ☐
I would like to subscribe to the newsletter: ☐

The checked attribute sets the box to active as a default selection.

Radio Buttons

A ChoiceMenu radio button represents groups of options. Within such a group, only a single option can be selected at a time. The \ChoiceMenu command requires the Form environment.

```
\begin{Form}
  \ChoiceMenu[radio, name=Age, radiosymbol=l]
            {Today I feel: }
             {old=o, young=y, neutral=n}
\end{Form}
```

Today I feel: old ☐ young neutral

There are many options available for the radiosymbol. The two most common options are: radiosymbol=4 (a tick in a square) and radiosymbol=l (a dot in a circle).

The selection options of a radio button group can also be arranged vertically. In this case, each individual option is created with its own ChoiceMenu. The association between them is defined via the name attribute. Options belonging to the same group must have the same value for this attribute.

```
\begin{Form}
  \begin{tabular}{lll}
   Today I feel
    & \ChoiceMenu[radio, name=Age2]{}{=o} & old.\\
  ~ & ~ & ~\\
  ~ & \ChoiceMenu[radio, name=Age2]{}{=y} & young.
 \end{tabular}
\end{Form}
```

Today I feel ☐ old.

☐ young.

Selection Lists

The ChoiceMenu command can also be used to create a selection list:

```
\begin{Form}
\ChoiceMenu[combo, name=Colour, width=3cm]                    ~
{Choose a colour: }{Red, Blue, Green, Yellow}
\end{Form}
```

Choose a colour:

Chapter 13

More Advanced Elements

This chapter covers some advanced techniques in LaTeX that go beyond the standard and allow for a deeper customisation of documents.

13.1 Some Very Helpful Packages

The microtype Package

The `microtype` package elevates a document's typography to a very high level. It optimises the spacing in justified text to avoid large white gaps (rivers), reduces the number of unsightly hyphenations at the end of a line, and ensures optical margin alignment by slightly protruding hyphens, commas, and quotation marks beyond the margin.

The cleveref Package

The `cleveref` package simplifies working with cross-references, as it automatically prefixes a reference with terms such as "Figure", "Table", "Equation", or "Page" (or their respective abbreviations) as appropriate. Consequently, these terms no longer need to be typed manually. The reference `\cpageref{sec-complex-tables}` thus refers to page 138, where section 13.4 (`\cref{sec-complex-tables}`) regarding complex table structures begins.

To ensure that `cleveref` uses the correct language, the package should be loaded with the appropriate language option (see `babel`):

```
\usepackage[english]{cleveref}
```

The following examples demonstrate the differences between \ref and \cref:

`fig. \ref{tikz-3}`	fig. 13.3
`\cref{tikz-3}`	fig. 13.3
`Figure \ref{tikz-1}`	Figure 13.1
`\Cref{tikz-1}`	Figure 13.1
`fig. \ref{tikz-2} und \ref{tikz-1}`	fig. 13.2 und 13.1
`\cref{tikz-2,tikz-1}`	figs. 13.1 and 13.2
`table \ref{tab1}`	table 13.1
`\cref{tab1}`	table 13.1
`eqs. (\ref{eq1}) bis (\ref{eq3})`	eqs. (13.1) bis (13.3)
`\cref{eq1,eq2,eq3}`	eqs. (13.1) to (13.3)

Here we also see the use of the \Cref command (with a capital C!) for a cross-reference at the beginning of a sentence, as abbreviations should not be used at the start of a sentence and a capital letter is required.

With the command \crefname{type}{singular}{plural} in the preamble, the words prefixed to the respective cross-references can be adjusted to suit your own requirements:

Figures	\crefname{figure}{fig.}{figs.}
Tables	\crefname{table}{table}{tables}
Equations	\crefname{equation}{equation}{equations}
Page number	\crefname{page}{p.}{pp.}

The same naturally applies to

\Crefname{type}{singular}{plural}.

The varioref package extends these possibilities even further. When including the packages varioref, hyperref, and cleveref, a specific order must be observed to avoid errors:

```
\usepackage[english]{varioref}
\usepackage[colorlinks=true,urlcolor=blue]{hyperref}
\usepackage[english]{cleveref}
```

The following examples demonstrate the results when using varioref and the \vref command:

\vref{tikz-3}	fig. 13.3 on page 142
\Vref{tikz-1}	Figure 13.1 on page 141
\vref{eq2}	eq. (13.2) on page 141
\vref{sec-classes}	section 13.2 on page 135

The csquotes Package

Using the csquotes package simplifies the inclusion of direct quotations. csquotes is responsible for automatically using the quotation marks that correspond to the language package selected with babel. It also detects when a quotation is nested within another and switches to the appropriate quotation marks for the "inner" quote. The csquotes package can also work in conjunction with the biblatex package.

A simple quotation within flowing text is created using the \enquote command. However, one should never forget to cite the source of the quotation:

```
No scientist begins their research without
prior knowledge. As \citeauthor{Newton-1675}
said as early as \citeyear{Newton-1675}:
\enquote{If I have seen further it is by standing
on the sholders of Giants.}
```

No scientist begins their research without prior knowledge. As Newton said as early as 1675: "If I have seen further it is by standing on the sholders of Giants."

For longer quotations spanning several lines, it is customary to indent them and omit quotation marks. In csquotes, this is implemented using the \blockquote{quoted text} command:

```
Regarding his scientific discoveries,
\textcite{Newton-1727} said:

\blockquote{I do not know what I may appear to
the world, but to myself I seem to have been only
like a boy playing on the sea-shore, and diverting
myself in now and then finding a smoother pebble
or a prettier shell than ordinary, whilst the great
ocean of truth lay all undiscovered before me.}
```

Regarding his scientific discoveries, Newton (1727) said:

> I do not know what I may appear to the world, but to myself I seem to have been only like a boy playing on the sea-shore, and diverting myself in now and then finding a smoother pebble or a prettier shell than ordinary, whilst the great ocean of truth lay all undiscovered before me.

Another example illustrates the use of nested quotations with `\enquote`:

```
\enquote{And then Marie said: \enquote{Nothing in
life is to be feared, it is only to be
understood. Now is the time to understand
more, so that we may fear less.} and
strolled into the sunset.}
```

"And then Marie said: 'Nothing in life is to be feared, it is only to be understood. Now is the time to understand more, so that we may fear less.' and strolled into the sunset."

The command sequence `\textquote[\cite{source}]{quotation}` enables the linking of a quotation with a bibliographic reference:

```
Thus, one of the most visionary sentences in the
history of technology comes from a female scientist:
\textquote[\cite{Lovelace-1843}]{The
Analytical Engine weaves algebraic patterns
just as the Jacquard loom weaves flowers and
leaves.}
```

Thus, one of the most visionary sentences in the history of technology comes from a female scientist: "The Analytical Engine weaves algebraic patterns just as the Jacquard loom weaves flowers and leaves." (Lovelace 1843)

13.2 Creating Custom Document Classes

Defining a custom **document class** is useful for developing a specific layout for a template that is intended to be reused regularly.

A document class is saved in a *cls* file (e.g. *myclass.cls*). If the document class file is located in the same directory as the document to be created using that class, the class can be used directly:

```
\documentclass{myclass}
```

The simplest way to create a custom document class is to build it based on an already existing class. In the following example, a custom document class is built upon the `scrartcl` class:

```
% myclass.cls
\ProvidesClass{myclass}[2026/02/12
              Custom document class]

% 1. Load the base class (scrartcl) with 12pt
% font size on A4 paper
\LoadClass[a4paper, 12pt]{scrartcl}

% 2. Load necessary packages
\RequirePackage{geometry}
\RequirePackage{xcolor}

% 3. Define layout settings
\geometry{
      margin=2.5cm,
      headheight=14pt
      }

% 4. Define new commands / variables
\newcommand{\myname}{Isaac Newton}
\definecolor{myblue}{RGB}{0, 51, 153}
```

The application in the main document then works as usual:

```
% Main document main.tex
\documentclass{myclass}

...

\begin{document}
\title{Project Documentation}
\author{\myname} % Uses the command defined
% in the class

\maketitle

...

\end{document}
```

13.3 Headers and Footers with fancyhdr

The `fancyhdr` package allows for the customisation of a document's headers and footers (Header: Head / Footer: Foot). This can be configured according to even (E) and odd (O) page numbers, with a further distinction between the Left (L), Centre (C), and Right (R) areas.

Once the `fancyhdr` package is included, the page style must be switched to the package's specifications in the preamble using:

```
\pagestyle{fancy}
```

The header and footer can now also be modified within the preamble:

```
% Header definition:
\fancyhead[position]{content}

% Footer definition:
\fancyfoot[position]{content}

% Header separator line definition:
\renewcommand{\headrulewidth}{X}

% Footer separator line definition:
\renewcommand{\footrulewidth}{X}
```

The position is composed of abbreviations that distinguish between even or odd page numbers (E or O) and left, centre, or right (L, C, or R) as the location. The definition

```
\fancyhead[OR]{\thepage}
\fancyhead[EL]{\thepage}
```

places the page number (\thepage) in the header on the right-hand margin (R) for odd pages (O) and on the left-hand margin (L) for even pages (E).

The following example demonstrates how headers and footers can be styled within the preamble:

```
...
\usepackage{fancyhdr}
\pagestyle{fancy} % Activates fancyhdr

% 1. Header for odd pages (outer right)
\fancyhead[RO]{\thepage}

% 2. Header for even pages (inner left)
\fancyhead[LE]{\nouppercase{\leftmark}}

% 3. Footer for all pages, centre:
\fancyfoot[C]{\footnotesize \copyright Jane
Doe}

% 4. Thickness of the separator line
\renewcommand{\headrulewidth}{0.4pt}
\renewcommand{\footrulewidth}{0.4pt}

% 5. Defines the plain style for pages that
% should have no header or footer, or a
% reduced version (e.g. the table of
% contents):
\fancypagestyle{plain}{
\fancyhead{} % Empty header for 'plain' pages
\renewcommand{\headrulewidth}{0pt}
}

\begin{document}
...
\end{document}
```

Several additional commands were used here: typically, titles in the header are set entirely in uppercase letters by default. The \nouppercase command changes this setting.

The plain style defined in the example is automatically used on various pages (e.g. the title page, the table of contents, or the first page of a chapter). On other pages, this style can be applied using the command:

```
\thispagestyle{plain}
```

The commands \leftmark and \rightmark output the titles of the current chapter and current section, respectively. These contents can be redefined using the command:

```
\markboth{LEFT}{RIGHT}
```

13.4 Table Design with tabularray

The tabularray package enables the creation of tables where design and content are separated. All formatting (alignment, rules, colours) is configured centrally at the beginning. Cells can be merged across multiple rows or columns without any difficulty. This is demonstrated in the following examples.

First, a simple example:

```
\begin{tblr}{
  colspec = {X[c]X[j]}, % Column 1: centred (c),
                        % Column 2: justified (j)
  hlines, vlines,       % All horizontal and
                        % vertical lines
  row{1} = {bg=violet, fg=white}, % Background colour
                                  % and font colour
                                  % in the first row
}
  ID & Description \\
  01 & This is a long text that is automatically
       wrapped within the cell. \\
  02 & In X-columns, the width is automatically
       calculated.\\
\end{tblr}
```

ID	Description
01	This is a long text that is automatically wrapped within the cell.
02	In X-columns, the width is automatically calculated.

And here is a second example demonstrating further possibilities. With Q-columns, the width can be set manually.

```
\begin{tblr}{
  colspec = {Q[c] Q[l,2cm] Q[c,2cm] Q[c,1cm]},
  hline{2} = {solid}, % Horizontal line BEFORE
                      % the 2nd row
  vline{2} = {solid}, % Vertical line BEFORE
                      % the 2nd column
}
  Head 1 & Head 2 & Head 3 & Head 4\\
  Cell 2.1 & \SetCell[c=2]{r} Horizontally merged
                                   (2 columns)
  & & Cell 2.4 \\
  Cell 3.1 & Cell 3.2 & Cell 3.3
      & \SetCell[r=2]{c} Vertically merged
                              (2 rows)\\
  Cell 4.1 & Cell 4.2 & Cell 4.3 &\\
  Cell 5.1 & Cell 5.2 & Cell 5.3 & Cell 5.4\\
  Cell 6.1 & Cell 6.2 & Cell 6.3 & Cell 6.4\\
\end{tblr}
```

Head 1	Head 2	Head 3	Head 4
Cell 2.1	Horizontally merged (2 columns)		Cell 2.4
Cell 3.1	Cell 3.2	Cell 3.3	Vertically merged (2 rows)
Cell 4.1	Cell 4.2	Cell 4.3	
Cell 5.1	Cell 5.2	Cell 5.3	Cell 5.4
Cell 6.1	Cell 6.2	Cell 6.3	Cell 6.4

The final example demonstrates the vertical alignment (`f`: bottom, `h`: top) of the cell content:

```
\begin{tblr}{
  colspec = {Q[l,h] Q[l,f] Q[l,h,2.5cm] Q[f]},
  hlines, vlines,
  row{1} = {bg=violet, fg=white}
}
  Head 1    & Head 2    & Head 3 & Head 4 \\\
  Cell 2.1  & Cell 2.2  & Cell 2.3 Cell 2.3
  Cell 2.3 & Cell 2.4 \\
  Cell 3.1  & Cell 3.2  & Cell 3.3 & Cell 3.4 \\
\end{tblr}
```

Head 1	Head 2	Head 3	Head 4
Cell 2.1	Cell 2.2	Cell 2.3 Cell 2.3 Cell 2.3	Cell 2.4
Cell 3.1	Cell 3.2	Cell 3.3	Cell 3.4

13.5 Section to Illustrate Working with the cleveref Package

This section does not offer any new content. The material is intended solely for working with the `cleveref` package in section 13.1.

$$f(x) = 2x^2 - 5x + 3 \tag{13.1}$$

$$g(x) = 3\sin(2x - 5) \tag{13.2}$$

$$h(x) = \frac{1}{2}(1 + \tanh(x)) \tag{13.3}$$

Spalte 1	Spalte 2	Spalte 3
Spalte 1	Spalte 2	Spalte 3
Spalte 1	Spalte 2	Spalte 3
Spalte 1	Spalte 2	Spalte 3

Table 13.1: A table as an example for the use of the *cleveref* package.

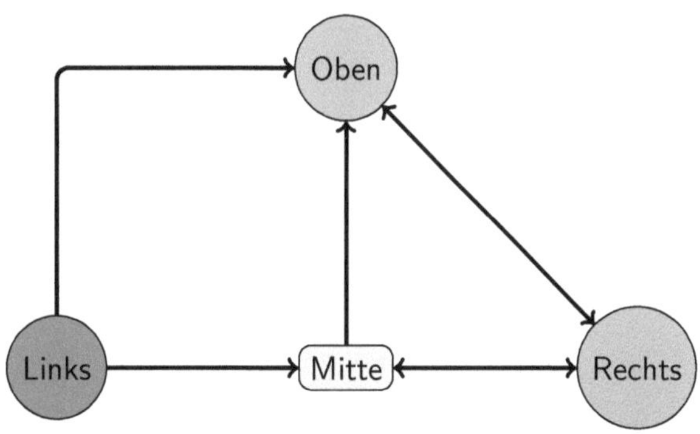

Figure 13.1: An image as an example for the use of the *cleveref* package.

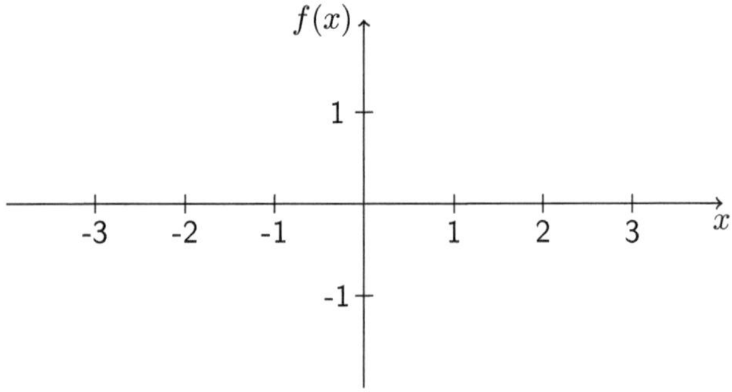

Figure 13.2: An image as an example for the use of the *cleveref* package.

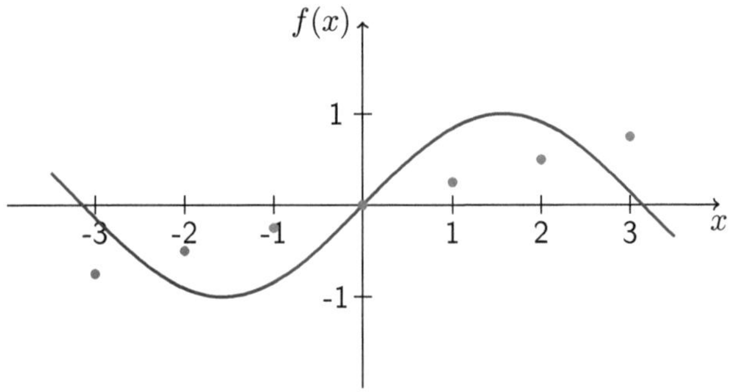

Figure 13.3: An image as an example for the use of the *cleveref* package.

Index